# The Second Journey

by
**Gerald O'Collins**

with

an afterword by

**Jack Dominian**

VILLA BOOKS
DUBLIN

Acknowledgements

Excerpts by C.J. Jung are taken from *Psychological Reflections,* edited by Jolande Jacobi and R.F.C. Hull, Bollingen Series XXXI, © 1970 by Princeton University Press. Material from *Face to Face: A Film* by Ingmar Bergman, translated by Alan Blair, © 1976 by Alan Blair, is reprinted by permission of Pantheon Books, a division of Random House, Inc. The excerpt from "The Road Not Taken" is taken from *The Poetry of Robert Frost,* edited by Edward Connery Lathem, copyright 1916, © 1969 by Holt, Rinehart and Winston, © 1944 by Robert Frost, and is reprinted by permission of Holt, Rinehart and Winston, Publishers. The excerpt from "Little Gidding" by T.S. Eliot is taken from *Four Quartets* and is reprinted by permission of Harcourt Brace Jovanovich, Inc. The excerpt from *Jesus Rediscovered* by Malcolm Muggeridge is reprinted by permission of Doubleday & Co., Inc.

This edition first published in 1979 by Villa Books Limited, 50 Upper O'Connell Street, Dublin 1 (for all countries outside Australia, Canada and the U.S.A.) and by Dove Communications Pty Limited, 203 Darling Road, East Malvern, Victoria 3145, Australia (for Australia only). Original edition published in 1978 by Paulist Press, New York.

ISBN 0 906408 10 5 (Villa Books)
ISBN 0 85924 117 3 (Dove Communications)

Printed and bound in Hong Kong

# Contents

*Preface*

Around midlife many people undergo a "second journey." This can be a thoroughly anxious and depressing experience, one that seems at times like a trip into idiotic meaninglessness.Identification of the experience may, however, help to disarm the terrors and bring some renewed assurance to those who see themselves in what follows.

Sister Bridget Puzon, O.S.U., created the term "second" or "midlife" journey, developed the theme in a 1973 Harvard University dissertation[1] and other studies, and in private conversations provided me with further ideas. I wish to acknowledge and thank her warmly for the initial thoughts on which I want now to build.

In *Passages*,[2] Gail Sheehy maintains: "Each of us stumbles upon the major issue of midlife somewhere in the decade between 35 and 45." Her own second journey began at 35 when she was covering a story in Northern Ireland. She was standing next to a young man when a bullet blew his face off. For the first time in her life she felt herself confronted with death and its approach—with what she calls "the arithmetic of life." She suddenly realized that *no one is with me. No one keeps me safe. There is no one who won't ever leave me alone.*

3

Bloody Sunday in Londonderry threw Ms. Sheehy off balance and flung at her a barrage of painful questions about her ultimate purposes and values. It need not be a bullet that initiates a second journey. A 35 year-old wife learns of her husband's infidelity. A 40 year-old company director finds that making money suddenly seems absurd. A 45 year-old journalist gets smashed up in a car accident. However it happens, such people feel confused and even lost. They can no longer keep life in working order. They are dragged away from chosen and cherished patterns to face strange crises. This is their second journey.

It has, of course, been a commonplace to describe human life as a journey and religious life as a pilgrimage. Nevertheless, we are not dealing with a single undifferentiated journey. It came as a shock to Gail Sheehy that "life after adolescence is *not* one long plateau." Jung makes the same point:

> Wholly unprepared, we embark upon the second half of life. Or are there perhaps colleges for forty-year-olds which prepare them for their coming life and its demands as the ordinary colleges introduce our young people to a knowledge of the world? No, thoroughly unprepared we take the step into the afternoon of life; worse still, we take this step with the false assumption that our truths and ideals will serve us as hitherto. But we cannot live the afternoon of life according to the programme of life's morning: for what in the morning was true will at evening have become a lie.[3]

Life is a series of different journeys. We need to distinguish one journey from another, if this image is going to succeed in enlightening us.

Taking up Sr. Puzon's identification of the phenomenon, this book aims to reflect further on second or midlife journeys. Human history is littered with instances: from John Wesley to Jimmy Carter, from Ignatius Loyola to Eleanor Roosevelt, from John Henry Newman to Dietrich Bonhoeffer. Western literature enshrines numerous examples of such second journeys. Works like the *Odyssey*, the *Aeneid* and Bunyan's *Pilgrim's Progress* present heroes driven in midlife to leave their familiar environ-

4

ment, attempt new projects and travel strange roads.[4] This is being "in the middle way," as T. S. Eliot put it in *East Coker*. The reader's mind may dart back to the *Inferno* and Dante's version of the mid-point journey. It does not seem to matter whether the image of the second journey derives from man's undoubted history or from his literary imagination. The formal gap between fiction and non-fiction disappears. The real world of such midlife journeys has created its make-believe counterpart which reflects and illuminates these journeys.

The theme of this book can be developed in three stages. First, the central image needs to be clarified. Then I will reflect on a number of cases of second journeys. From these some characteristic patterns may emerge. Finally, I plan to make several suggestions about ways of coping with second journeys.

Many people may find the book an unnecessary piece of mystification. Why not simply write straight psycho-history and leave out the piety and cant? Some religiously dedicated people may think that the work fails to come out in the open. Why not, for instance, give full attention to the particular struggles faced on second journeys by those who have chosen a vocational life as nuns, ministers, priests, rabbis, missionaries and brothers?

To the first group, I would say this. We must seek to understand our lives at depth. We can try to push away ultimate questions about the meaning of it all. But to remove the mystery of human existence at one point is to find it coming back at another. For their part, the second group may need to recognize that their lives are not after all so "special." In particular, the second journeys of religiously dedicated people can parallel astonishingly the lives of lay people.

I should admit at least this much difference between the two groups. Religiously dedicated people of all kinds and denominations must face up to ultimate questions *as a matter of routine*. For them the onslaught of a journey-crisis can be doubly distressing and acute, if at least open to being better understood. In journey language—the way may be lost but the terrain is not totally unfamiliar. The drama for laymen and laywomen is the shock of an experience they scarcely understand and *may never identify at all*. The inner restlessness of a second journey may be agonized over by the religious group but risk being put down simply to exhaustion or depression by the other group. A laywoman on a second journey put it this way: "We all know the prescribed cures—holidays, health resorts, tranquilizers, gymnastics, vegetarianism and the rest."

This book is offered to both groups and to all who see themselves reflected in Dante's words:

> Nel mezzo del cammin di nostra vita
>     mi ritrovai per una selva oscura
>     che la diritta via era smarrita.

> (In the middle of our life's road
>     I found myself in a dark wood—
>     the straight way ahead lost.)

The image of the second journey is a piece of good news which should be shared with others. It is a symbol which can make sense of their spiritual psycho-history for countless men and women.

I dedicate this book to the Sisters of Mercy who form the Crispin Street Community in London's East End. Their work for homeless people, disadvantaged children, lonely old persons and the sick suggests those wider possibilities of human love to which a second journey might lead us.

I would like to express my sincere thanks to several people who must remain anonymous. They have allowed me to use their stories as cases illustrating a midlife journey. Some details have been changed to conceal their identities. I hope they will feel rewarded by the help they will undoubtedly bring to others. Personally, I felt immensely touched by their confidences and grateful for the wisdom they shared with me. I want also to thank my friend, Ravi Santosh Kamath, S.J., who kindly typed part of this manuscript. Finally, my thanks are due to many people in Rome, England, Germany, the United States and Australia whose reflections clarified my thinking on the theme of this book.

Gerald O'Collins
The Gregorian University
Rome, June 16, 1977

# Chapter One
## Sorting Out Our Journeys

The archetypes are the great decisive forces, they bring about the real events, and not our personal reasoning and practical intellect . . . The archetypal images decide the fate of man.

C. G. Jung

In September 1975, Ingmar Bergman wrote a letter to his cast and crew before they began filming *Face to Face*. He explained how the main character (Dr. Jenny Isaksson) had taken shape in the script he had prepared: "A well-adjusted, capable and disciplined person, a highly qualified professional woman with a career, comfortably married to a gifted colleague and surrounded by what are called 'the good things of life.' It is this admirable character's shockingly quick breakdown and agonizing rebirth that I have tried to describe."[1]

A little later in his letter, Bergman dropped the image of a "rebirth" and spoke briefly of Jenny's "voyage of discovery." It is this journey language that we can profitably develop and exploit. As we shall see, Jenny looks like a classic example of a second journey.

But first things first. We need to situate the second journey in relation to the "first" and "third" journeys of life.

## I

### SETTLING DOWN

The *first* journey is *the whole movement* from childhood through adolescence to adulthood.[2] That journey involves passing through the challenges and crises of two decades to find a measure of emotional stability and at least some provisional identity.

In the light of the values we are taught, we define some meaningful existence and give ourselves to it. We make firm commitments—a commitment in marriage or, for a small minority, the commitment to a religious life. We take our place in the world.

Success can build up our self-confidence. We prove our competence and achieve things as a business man, a teacher, a parent, a nursing sister, a politician or a priest. We find that we are earning our credentials from our firm, our family, our diocese. Others approve of us. Society rewards us. Perhaps we reach pretty quickly the goals we—consciously or unconsciously—set for ourselves. We become the principal of a school, a successful social worker, the head of some department, the rabbi in charge of a large synagogue.

It often happens that this first journey entails much insecurity and deep searching before we find release from teenage fears and incoherence. It may take a great deal of self-examination to fashion our values. There can be severe crises in accepting "shoulds," settling our commitments, achieving successes and finding our identity.

In his letter to the cast and crew, Bergman called Jenny Isaksson "a stifling, static combination of mapped-out qualities and patterns of behaviour." In the story itself, Jenny puts it this way: "We act the play. We learn our lines. We know what people want us to say. We lie. In the end it's not even deliberate." She calls herself "capable" and "conscientious." "You can rely on Jenny. Just as if she were something real. An airplane engine or a rowboat." She bursts out and recalls how her grandmother brought her up after her parents died:

You can't wear that dress today. It's your Sunday best. You'll never manage that, my dear. Let me help you. Using lipstick are you? Most unseemly while you're living in our home. Eat up what you have on your plate. You're late again. Will you never learn to be punctual? You're lazy and

10

spoiled. If you go on like this, Grandpa and I will send you to boarding school, you'll soon learn to mend your ways there, my girl.

Punishment reinforced the demand to accept all the "shoulds" and "don'ts." Her grandmother hit Jenny across the face and locked her in a closet. "Can you imagine shutting up a child who's afraid of the dark in a closet?"

Jenny is a frightening, if common, example of the way the first journey often goes. Parents or others threaten, nag, punish and exhort—all for the purpose of shaping our behavior and directing us towards "success."

Some pass through that first journey with less pain. We can term such people the "smooth evolvers." They accept their "shoulds" easily enough from others. They take over or find their values without much fuss, give themselves to a line of action and find some provisional identity—the goal of the first journey.

Whether they happen painfully or peacefully, all first journeys leave some questions open. Have these persons found a real center? Have they reached a genuine integrity and final identity? Or are they, like Jenny, the "successful" psychiatrist who eventually attempts suicide and asks the doctor who saves her: "Do you think I'm crippled for the rest of my life? Do you think we're a vast army of emotionally crippled wretches wandering about calling to each other with words which we don't understand and which only make us even more afraid?" Let me hasten to add that it would be misleading and even demonstrably mistaken to take Jenny—not to mention those other heroines and heroes of Bergman's films who tremble constantly on the brink of insanity—as anything like a "normal" example. Chapter two will reflect on several much more cheerful cases of people who have undergone second journeys and do not feel the need to describe their experiences in such extreme and desolate language.

Of course, it may seem neither satisfying nor useful to describe as a first journey everything that a person passes through from birth to the mid or late twenties. Freud and his successors have given us an array of psychological terms with which to map the various developmental stages in children and teenagers. Ultimately, it will be a matter of taste (in the deepest sense of that word). We can split up the first two decades of human life into a number of discrete, if interrelated, segments. Or we may prefer to see those years as forming *one great trajectory*, the first journey.

Journey language has at least one clear advantage here. Normally, by their late twenties men and women have moved from their parental homes to marry, to take a house or an apartment and set up on their own, or (in the case of a tiny minority of Christians) to live in a religious community. Literally, most people make a physical journey when they grow up. They move to some new and self-chosen place where they settle down.

Society tolerates immature behavior from the teenager and permits the twenty-year-old to "sow wild oats." A kind of "Grand Tour" still forms part of the first journey which society caters to. But when young men and women take a permanent job, reach marriage, get ordained or take final vows, it is all now meant to be such a straight run through the late twenties, the thirties and right on to one's retirement in the sixties. The predictable crises of the first journey are over: puberty, leaving school, completing novitiate, finishing basic training programs and the rest. After this first journey society allows only for what I call the third journey.

## II
### ONE LAST JOURNEY

The third journey involves aging and moving through the last years before death.[3] This journey too can have clear outer landmarks: leaving some lifelong job, a shift to a retirement village or nursing home, the death of a spouse, going to live with one's married daughter.

Not everyone takes part in this third journey. By definition, those struck down by death in youth or middle-age make no such journey. But millions do endure what Shakespeare terms the sixth and seventh "ages" of man.

> The sixth age shifts
> Into the lean and slipper'd pantaloon,
> With spectacles on nose and pouch on side,
> His youthful hose, well saved, a world too wide
> For his shrunk shank; and his big manly voice,
> Turning again toward childish treble, pipes
> And whistles in his sound. Last scene of all,
> That ends this strange eventful history,
> Is second childishness and mere oblivion,
> Sans teeth, sans eyes, sans taste, sans everything.
>
> *(As You Like It*, Act II, Scene 7.)

When physical powers fail, we need few reminders that we are mortal. The mournful brightness of memory recalls the lost days of strength and youth. Our restless minds can wonder whether life will truly be renewed beyond death. No painter or poet surpasses Rembrandt in representing this third journey. With the utmost sensitivity and compassion, his self-portraits trace the purging of a human spirit in the final years of its earthly life.

In his *Jesus Rediscovered*, Malcolm Muggeridge highlights the special beauty and simplicity of those last years. Quite naturally he reaches for the language of a journey:

> I am old, and in at most a decade or so will be dead. . . . The prospect of death overshadows all others. I am like a man on a sea voyage nearing his destination. When I embarked I worried about having a cabin with a porthole, whether I should be asked to sit at the Captain's table, who were the more attractive and important passengers. All such considerations become pointless when I shall so soon be disembarking. As I do not believe that earthly life can bring any lasting satisfaction, the prospect of death holds no terrors. Those saints who pronounced themselves in love with death displayed, I consider, the best of sense.[4]

13

Whatever elderly people make of their situation, their third journey—like the first journey—enjoys one comforting advantage: There are millions of fellow-travellers on the road just ahead. On the first journey, many changes can arrive more or less on schedule: puberty, leaving school, graduation and the rest. At times girls and boys find it impossible to share their parents' enthusiasm for what they have to go through. All the same, even if they never read scientific studies on the human predicament of the teenager, they are normally surrounded by many peers going through similar experiences. These others provide living models for those following behind them. In short, the shifts and moves of the first journey are often pretty predictable. Likewise, the stages of a third journey—from the crisis of retirement on—can often be readily predicted. Generally, one is surrounded by hundreds of people going through identifiably similar predicaments. The sense of shared experience can make all the difference.

The second journey, however, has an unpredictable quality about it. It can come as a sudden shock that life after the first journey "is *not* one long plateau" (Gail Sheehy). We may find ourselves "wholly unprepared" (Jung) as we move into our midlife journey. But what does a second journey involve? Some provisional account can be given here before we look at several cases.

### III
#### IN THE MIDDLE WAY

Men and women called on a second journey suffer a loss of orientation. Their first journey seemed to have settled their situation, but now things turn uncertain. Their social identity appeared happily established, but now they leave their "normal" roles to face and accept unexpected challenges.[5] The group consensus no longer satisfies them. They feel compelled to make another experiment with life. They want to evaluate everything anew and try themselves out again.

This second journey is a voyage of self-exploration which

can help people really discover themselves in the mid-years of their lives. "Mid-years" should not be taken too narrowly. Second journeys can occur at almost any stage: from the late twenties to the fifties or even into the sixties. If the "second journey" terminology expresses the events of innumerable human lives, such a journey also repeats itself in countless myths. The figure of Ulysses embraces not only the second journey (the *Odyssey*) but a first and third journey as well. On his first journey he becomes a suitor of Helen, settles down with Penelope, begets a son, and rules Ithaca until he reluctantly joins the expedition to Troy. Twenty years of his midlife pass before Ulysses gets home. Tennyson adds a third journey to the story of the Greek hero. The aged Ulysses "cannot rest from travel." He leaves his "sceptre and the isle" to his son, "mine own Telemachus," and sails away on one last journey:

Old age hath yet his honour and his toil;
Death closes all: but something ere the end,
Some work of noble note, may yet be done . . .
> for my purpose holds
To sail beyond the sunset, and the baths
Of all the western stars, until I die.

> (*Ulysses*)


## IV
### THREE DIFFICULTIES

Right at the outset it is as well to face three difficulties. First, will "second journey" talk turn out to be just another abstraction or abridgement which simplifies many different and distinct human stories into one overgeneralized pattern? Experience varies from person to person. Can we come up with some standard structure or fixed set of basic experiences to which everyone is supposed to conform? Each of us seems to take in a somewhat different world and then, prodded by our needs, desires and evaluations, does "our own thing." Will it help to launch "second journey" terminology into discussion? Every generalized description of human beings in their endless variety must, I suppose, face this objection. The concrete particulars get left behind, just as they are in Freud's psychological language or in evangelical talk about being "born again." Ultimately, the reading public must decide whether the image of the second journey throws light on their individual experiences. Only they can judge whether this symbol merely generalizes a number of particular cases or truly represents a discovery of something more or less universal. They can tell whether the "second journey" genuinely mirrors the human condition or simply accounts for some special or even extreme cases.

The second objection resembles the first. Does the scheme of first, second and third journeys amount to an improvement on—or at least a real alternative to—existing schemes? I think here of Erik Erikson's eight stages of human life, George Vaillant's use of "second adolescence," or the language of "midlife crisis" which Gail Sheehy and others have taken over from Elliott Jaques' paper, "Death and the Mid-Life Crisis" (1965).

A full-scale defense of the second journey image would involve us in a thorough examination of all other major schemes for describing human life—from Shakespeare's seven stages of man and the three "ways" of medieval mysticism (purgative, illuminative and unitive) down to Erikson's eight stages and Miss Sheehy's set of "passages." Let me at least say this. "Midlife crisis" sounds just a little too negative. We hear of "the energy crisis," the recurrent "Middle East crisis," some "schools crisis" or a "crisis in seminary vocations." We probably wish that such awkward—to put it mildly—crises in our economic, political, educational and religious life were not there. Of course, someone will always remind us that, after all, such crises may turn out to be challenges to a false status quo and opportunities for future growth and true renewal. Nevertheless, no amount of coaxing will take away the negative and gloomy aura which clings to the word "crisis." One way or another, any crisis threatens to rip our life apart at the seams. It suggests primarily a menace.

"Second adolescence" sounds like a put-down. Against Vaillant's best intentions, the term inevitably sells short what happens when some 45 year-old man suddenly finds it hard to continue his role as father and breadwinner, lapses into some sexual adventure and looks for a completely new job. Is he simply regressing to the storm and fury of an emotionally unstable young man? Speaking of "second adolescence" seems only a step away from telling someone, "Stop acting like a teenager!" Let me hasten to add that I do not wish to excuse and bless everything that people do on a second journey. Such a journey is no self-justifying activity. It is a challenge leading to diverse possibilities, one being the choice of a *counterfeit destination*. Nevertheless, respect for the portentous nature of what is happening should warn us against trivializing matters by using the wrong terminology.

All in all, "second journey" has a much more positive ring to it. It is not just an image, but a guiding image. Admittedly, a journey can imply risks and dangers. Nevertheless, the power of positive thinking clings to the phrase. A journey sounds at least moderately attractive. We instinctively shy away from a crisis—certainly one entailing a second adolescence. Admittedly, it would be absurd to drop the word crisis from our vocabulary. That would be an unnecessary and quite curious piece of self-denial. But it is quite another thing to make "midlife crisis" one's central point of reference.

The third difficulty with the "journey" terminology may be this. Does the design cut up the whole of a given human life into three segments, so that a person who lives to the age of seventy might spend twenty-five years on the first journey, thirty on the second and fifteen on the third? Not at all. After their first journey *ends*, people reap the fruit of it. By twenty-five a man or woman can have come to provisional identity and found a place in which to settle down. Their first journey is completed. A second journey, if they experience one, may begin only ten or twenty years later. The termination of the first and the start of the second journey can be widely separated in time. Likewise, the second journey can close years before the third journey—that final pilgrimage towards death—begins. Decades of wise and fruitful living may intervene between the completion of the second journey and the onset of the third.

But it is high time to get down some cases to illustrate what second journeys look like in the concrete. Ultimately, it is the reading public who must take sides and determine whether this journey terminology has the effect of making the experience it describes less threatening and more intelligible.

# Chapter Two
# Getting Down Some Cases

To live is to change and to be perfect is to have changed often.

John Henry Newman

It was a new sense of release and assurance and peace with myself and a genuine interest in other people that I hadn't experienced before.

Jimmy Carter

$A$ compulsive quoting of cases could turn this chapter into a filing cabinet. Yet the image of a second journey will not prove sharp nor quickly etch its point in the reader's mind, unless we review some cases from the past and the present. The factors that trigger off a second journey suggest ways of grouping the stories.


I

A SENSE OF FAILURE


Some notable personal failure can initiate a transformation of consciousness in the middle years. John Wesley (1703–91) and Jimmy Carter exemplify a second journey which starts in this way.

For his ordination in 1728, Wesley returned to Oxford where he joined a group which critics named The Holy Club. The Reforming Club, Bible Moths, Methodists and Enthusiasts. "Methodists" was the name which would stick. In his late twenties, Wesley carried out his resolution to be "an altogether

Christian," one "all-devoted to God."[1] Several books fed his desire to seek perfection and genuine holiness: Thomas à Kempis' *The Imitation of Christ*, Jeremy Taylor's *Exercises of Holy Living and Dying* and two works by William Law (*Christian Perfection* and *A Serious Call to a Devout and Holy Life*). Taylor's teaching about "purity of intention" prompted a strong commitment:

> Instantly I resolved to dedicate *all my life* to God, *all* my thoughts and words and actions, being thoroughly convinced that there was no medium but that *every* part of my life (not some only) must either be a sacrifice to God or to myself.

Wesley started to keep a rule of life based on Taylor:

1. Begin and end every day with God: and sleep not immoderately.
2. Be diligent in your calling.
3. Employ all spare hours in religion; as able.
4. [Observe] all holidays (holy days).
5. Avoid drunkards and busybodies.
6. Avoid curiosity, and all useless employments and knowledge.
7. Examine yourself every night.
8. Never on any account pass a day without setting aside at least an hour for devotion.
9. Avoid all manner of passion.

Both before and after Wesley, one can find countless examples of similar rules of life adopted with the generosity of youth. Many young nuns, students for the ministry and newly-ordained priests long to get on with a dedicated life. They sternly adhere to a daily program and a set of resolutions which they have fashioned for themselves or drawn from the rules of their religious order or congregation.

For that matter, not a few married couples also elaborate their high standards, put together some weekly or even daily program, and vigorously give themselves to such a quest for success. "We wanted ours to be the perfect marriage," one such couple told me. Their marriage had started exceedingly well and after some years turned into a mess. Yet, like Wesley, they illustrate the kind of moves made by idealists when they reach the end of the first journey. They have defined the meaning of life, fixed their values and found an identity. Now they commit themselves generously to a clear course of action. Some carry through their programs as Wesley did. He described his ministry in Oxford as follows:

In 1730 I began visiting the prisons; assisting the poor and sick in town: and doing what other good I could, by my presence or my little fortune to the bodies and souls of all men. To this end I abridged myself of all superfluities and many that are called necessities of life. I soon became a by-word for so doing, and I rejoiced that my name was cast out as evil. The next spring I began observing the Wednesday and Friday fasts, commonly observed in the ancient church; tasting no food till three in the afternoon. And now I knew not how to go any further. I diligently strove against all sin. I omitted no sort of self-denial which I thought lawful; I carefully used, both in public and private, all the means of grace at all opportunities. I omitted no occasion of doing good; I for that reason suffered evil. And all this I knew to be nothing, unless as it was directed toward inward holiness. Accordingly this, the image of God, was what I aimed at in all, by doing his will, not my own. Yet when after continuing some years in this course I apprehended myself to be near death, I could not find that all this gave me any comfort or any assurance of acceptance with God.

In late 1735, Wesley sailed for Georgia with his brother and two friends. He felt frustrated. Missionary work among the North American Indians, he hoped, would help him to realize the ideals of Christian perfection he had set for himself. Instead, the shift from a fixed place in his society was to bring a transformation of consciousness.

The mission to the Indians turned out to be a wretched failure. Wesley fell in love with an 18 year-old girl, who proceeded to elope with a rival suitor. Wesley barred her from Holy Communion, and faced a court action brought by her new husband. After two years in Georgia, he sailed back to England discredited and desperate—full of "fearfulness and heaviness," as he put it. In his disgust at himself and the world, he even considered giving up preaching. Then, a few months after his return, he went "very unwillingly" to a prayer meeting in London. While someone read from Luther's preface to St. Paul's letter to the Romans, Wesley knew his heart to be "strangely warmed" and felt some of that assurance about salvation he had hungered for. He moved quickly to initiate a powerful religious movement. The decisive first decade (1739–49) of Methodist Revival was on the way.

Failure and an outer journey proved catalysts of change for Wesley. Of course, other factors contributed to his second journey. But the outer landmarks of travel—from an Oxford ministry to a fiasco in Georgia and back to an unexpected experience in London—marked the decisive stages of an inner progress which created a new life for Wesley.

From 1738, Wesley enjoyed a wiser and freer way of life. With prodigal energy he gave himself to reshaping the Christian community of the country he had left in frustration just a few years earlier. He worked tirelessly for the working classes being created by the Industrial Revolution. Lecky was to argue that the ministry of Wesley saved England from horrors like the Reign of Terror in the French Revolution. Wesley preached 40,000 sermons, published 50 volumes in his *Christian Library*, supported William Wilberforce in his fight against the slave trade, and at his death in 1791 left behind 70,000 disciples in Britain and 15,000 in America. In the aftermath of his second journey, Wesley proved an extraordinarily creative agent for people's spiritual growth. He gave full play to the impulse to be a mentor and pass on to others what he had happily experienced himself. Those who appreciate Erik Erikson's terminology will dub this development "generativity," a concern to hand on to the next generation what one believes to be valuable.

In short, Wesley's second journey let him come to himself, find a fresh equilibrium and experience a power that enabled him to fashion a new and enduring community.

Jimmy Carter's second journey also involved the state of Georgia. This journey took place in his early forties, rather than the thirties, as was the case with Wesley. But it was like Wesley's in being born of personal failure and disappointment.

In September 1966, Jimmy Carter lost the Democratic primary election for the governorship of Georgia. He was then 41 years old. The margin was only 20,000 votes out of the million or so ballots cast. This setback led to what Carter and others have called a "born-again" experience. It looks like an obvious case of a second journey.

After his defeat, Carter heard a sermon entitled "If You Were Arrested for Being a Christian, Would There Be Enough Evidence to Convict You?" He felt his answer could only be "No." Yet the sermon set him moving. Ten years later, in a television interview, he explained to Bill Moyers:

I was going through a state in my life then that was a very difficult one. I had run for governor and lost. Everything I did was not gratifying. When I succeeded in something, it was a horrible experience for me. I'd never done much for other people. I was always thinking about myself.

But then something happened.

I changed somewhat for the better. I formed a much more intimate relationship with Christ. And since then, I've had just about like a new life. As far as hatreds, frustrations, I feel at ease with myself.

Carter's sister, Ruth Stapleton, recalls that in late 1966 she went walking with him in the woods. "I talked about my awareness of Christ, and I shared with Jimmy how it was to come to a place of total commitment, the peace and the joy and the power it brings." She asked whether he was willing to surrender everything for Christ, even politics. He shrank from answering "Yes."

Ruth urged that if he could not do that, he would never enjoy peace. He broke down and wept.

Shortly afterwards Carter went off and did lay missionary work in Pennsylvania and Massachusetts. He spent one week in May 1967 with an older missionary, whose sincerity succeeded in converting a dozen or more families of non-believers. In an interview, Carter spoke of those days:

> The whole week was almost a miracle to me and I felt the sense of the presence of God's influence in my life. I called my wife on the phone one night and she said, "Jimmy, you don't sound like the same person. You sound almost like you're intoxicated . . ." And I said, "Well, in a way I am . . ." It was a new sense of release and assurance and peace with myself and a genuine interest in other people that I hadn't experienced before. I felt then and ever since that when I meet each individual person, they are important to me. I found myself able to say, "What can I do to make this other person's life even more enjoyable?"—even people that I met on an elevator or in a chance encounter on the street. In the past, I had a natural inclination to say, "What can I get from them?" Or, to wipe them out of my mind. Now it's just a different feeling altogether.[2]

In his own way Carter shows the truth of Yeats' observation, "Perhaps nothing can be sole or whole that has not been rent."

When we sort out what Carter's second journey entailed, several points emerge:

1. An unpleasant and unwanted defeat set this second journey going.

2. Ruth Stapleton confirms what in any case we would guess. Carter was deeply upset and emotionally thrown off balance.

3. An outer journey formed the context in which an interior journey took place.

4. He ceased to define himself by winning. In learning to live with failure and love others, he found new values by which to commit himself.

26

5. Carter's self-discovery and fresh purposes gave an energetic impetus to his life.

Whether Carter's coming to himself in his mid-years will truly and fully illustrate Erikson's principle of generativity remains, of course, to be seen. To put it mildly, history has still to record and interpret his contribution.

Besides John Wesley and Jimmy Carter, plenty of other cases suggest themselves where a personal failure seems to have triggered off a second journey. One thinks of John Profumo, Britain's Secretary of State for War, caught sharing his girl friend with a Russian Embassy military attaché. At the age of 48 he abruptly had to break off his parliamentary career. He turned to working for the poor and disadvantaged in London's East End.

The image of a second journey allows what Wesley, Carter and Profumo went through to fall into place. These cases may seem larger than life or even extreme. But they appear to be symptomatic of what many people experience—macrocosms to lots of microcosms.

Speaking of these and other cases as "macrocosms" could be misleading. I shrink from any suggestion that I set all these people and their stories on anything like the same level of importance. They illustrate a common pattern without necessarily enjoying a similar value for mankind.


## II
### EXILE

A further catalyst for a midlife journey is exile. Dante is a classic instance. Exiled from Florence, he was in his forties when he began his great work, *The Divine Comedy*, which embodied the vision of a journey through hell, purgatory and paradise.

In the middle of our life's road
I found myself in a dark wood—
the straight way ahead lost.

The lines suggest fear, lostness and an uneasy sense of inner collapse. Dante had crossed the frontier between growing up and growing old. He continued to share existence with others ("our life"). Yet he was alone ("I found myself").

Loneliness seems to mark all second journeys. Yet it bears down especially heavily on exiled and "displaced" persons, as well as on voluntary migrants. These travellers endure solitary trials—far from home, peace and company. This is not to say that *all* migrants and exiled people pass through a midlife journey. To point out the obvious: Many such persons may be too old or too young for such an experience. But the image of a second journey can make sense of what countless men and women have gone through: Jews who fled the Hitler regime, migrants to the United States or such a figure as Daniel Mannix (1864–1963). Mannix served as president of St. Patrick's College, Maynooth (Ireland) from 1903 to 1912, when he became an archbishop in Australia. Writers have puzzled and argued over some changes in the attitudes he showed in Dublin and then later in Melbourne. But did his personality and values have to be set in concrete by the late forties? Could it be that an inner journey accompanied the voyage to Australia?

The fact that it is Dante who has provided the classic statement on the second journey should make us more willing to recognize such journeys when people freely migrate or are forced into exile. Those government officials in my own country, who encouraged the public after the Second World War to call migrants "New Australians," spoke truer than they thought. Many of the adults among these migrants undoubtedly came through emotional upset, loneliness and a quest for fresh values to a new life, in which they found a lasting stability at the end of their second journey.

### III
### LOVE AND ANGER

Another set of second journeys cluster together under the heading of "love and anger." From our late twenties we can be absorbed in our careers and concerns. We may protect ourselves from facing our own emotions. Proven competence and public success can keep us blind to some real needs or block us from raising and settling questions about whole sectors of our life. Eventually, suffocated feelings of resentment or a hunger for intimacy may simply erupt from the depths of an outraged nature. Or—to vary the metaphor—love and anger can strip away whole layers of protective covering to let us start moving in a midlife journey, which is ultimately a coming to ourselves. "Real" life and literature offer endless examples of such second journeys which are fashioned by the push of anger and the pull of love.

In Bergman's novel and film *Face to Face,* Jenny Isaksson shifts houses for the summer. Her outward journey is slight, just a few miles from one home to another. But it brings her to live with her grandparents and to confront the pain which her grandmother caused her as a child. For years Jenny has spent her energy in working superbly for others, while denying or manipulating her own feelings. "I've followed the principle that now I'll make up my mind to feel like this and I feel like this." The end of this "lifelong illness" is terrifying. "At last," she admits, "there's only a puppet left, reacting more or less to external demands and stimuli. Inside there is nothing but a great horror."

But a friend (Tomas) helps Jenny to face the pain she had suffered as a child. She accepts the limitations of humanity and attains a kind of tender wisdom. In knowing herself she can reach out to others in new ways. Her self-discovery liberates her to face the world again. Significantly, Bergman turns to journey language indicating the chance given to Jenny—the paradox of a movement towards herself which will also bring her back to others. "If . . . she accepts her knowledge, she lets herself be drawn farther and farther in toward the center of her universe, guided by the light of intuition, a voyage of discovery which at the same time opens her up to the other people." What Jenny experiences is nothing more nor less than a second journey.

Another example. In his *A Question of Conscience* (1967), Charles Davis set out his reasons for leaving the Roman Catholic Church at the age of forty-three. The decision of this theolo-

29

gian shocked Catholics in England and elsewhere. Davis had attended the third session of the Vatican Council, been a successful editor of the *Clergy Review*, and proved a popular teacher in the United Kingdom and the United States. One journalist spoke of his departure as the most important event for the English Catholic Church since Newman's conversion in 1845.

In his apologia, Professor Davis recalled the dedication with which for over twenty years he had "worked in the Church as a priest, wedded to the ministry, immersed in theology and ecclesiastical matters, absorbed in Church concerns." Then in the mid-sixties, he found it necessary for his "integrity and freedom," to leave the institutional Church. "From the depths of my being," he explained, "I wanted to be freed from a system which was oppressing and tormenting me." As he put it elsewhere, "One of the factors that drove me from the Catholic Church was the unhappiness I met within it, and I was caught up myself in the destructive tensions that at present mark its life." Two basic motives shaped his move: repugnance at an institution in which he had completed his first journey and to which he had given his best, and the pull of love. "I am marrying," he stated, "to rebuild my life upon a personal love I can recognize as true and real, after a life surrounded in the Church by so much that is at best irrelevant and at worst an obstacle to genuine human experience."

The image of a second journey pulls together different elements in the story of Charles Davis: his outer journeyings to Rome and elsewhere, his pain and outrage at the Roman Catholic Church as both "a sea of unhappiness" and "a zone of untruth, pervaded by a disregard for truth," and his desire to "rebuild" and find peace through "the liberating power of a woman's love." His identity had been established as a popular teacher and writer. But he felt driven to leave his community of shared beliefs. The solutions at hand in the Catholic Church could no longer hold him. He moved from his position in English society to settle eventually in Montreal.

Father A. offers a further example of someone driven into a second journey by anger at an institution (the Catholic Church) and hunger for the fresh start offered by marriage. This English-speaking priest has let me use a letter which he intended to send to his bishop. Let me quote the document at length.

Dear Bishop X:
As you have been for so many years such a good friend, it makes it all the more difficult to write this letter to you. I am writing to ask you to apply to Rome for a dispensation from my priestly obligations. I have decided to leave the ministry, take a position as a teacher and get married. I know this decision will be very hurtful and disappointing to you and many other people. But it seems to me that I cannot keep saying and doing things that I experience as meaningless or worse, simply because I desire to please others or at least not to cause them sorrow . . . The personal experiences which lie behind this decision are very many, as old as school experiences and as new as the Pope's encyclical on birth control. Perhaps the best thing to do is to set out the reasons for my decision, adding data from my personal history where these seem relevant.
*Reasons for Decision.* First, I no longer accept the dogmas of papal infallibility, infallibility of the Church Councils, inerrancy of scripture, the Immaculate Conception and the Assumption, nor do I accept much of the Church's juridical structure. On almost all points I would agree with Charles Davis, apart from his decision to leave the Church . . . Since 1966 I have been conscious of how I was trying to defend the indefensible in arguing for the above dogmas. I want the freedom to think about and express openly my faith and that of other Christians both past and present, without feeling an institutional obligation to be loyal to the "party line." In the Church's official teaching (see, for example, Pope Paul's recent "Credo of the People of God") I find for the most part an outdated superstructure obscuring the simplicity and deep demands of the gospel.
At the time of his departure I was critical of Charles Davis' stress on truth ᵃⁿᵈ reasons, notions that recur over

and over again in his *Observer* article on 1 January 1967. I felt that he had wrongly emphasised the Christian mind at the expense of the Christian heart. But hasn't the appeal to love, humility and trustful submission been so often a means of covering up falsity and deceit? Our Lord had a most loving heart, but he was also adamant in the defence of truth. I think that Catholic theology has so often been corrupted and inhibited because in blind loyalty it has taken on the burden of defending Popes and Councils at all costs. I see the ill effect of this false loyalty even on such a great theologian as Karl Rahner. If I do not accept papal infallibility and the other dogmas mentioned above, I do not see what place I have in the Catholic priesthood.

Second, I want to live a life based on the New Testament. This means for me trying to understand the gospel message, looking at the Church and the world, evaluating what I am and what I can do, finding some role for the Church and the world that is meaningful personally and worth giving my life for, and deciding on that. I find the official Church still so crippled by law and lacking in the genuine spirit of Christian freedom and joy. I don't want to leave the Church, but on the other hand I don't want dishonestly to engage myself as part of the official Church's machinery.

Third, evaluating myself means above all facing the issue of celibacy. This is *actuel* for me in the sense that I have become very fond of a French woman whom I met last year. Increasingly the appropriate relationship of a celibate Catholic priest to women has become very difficult for me. . .

*The Future.* My reflections, prayer, reading of scripture and discussions with my confessor led me to put a question which has been constantly with me during the past month: Shall I give my life back to God as a whole life, or as a mutilated, partly unnatural, inhuman life? I realize how exaggerated that can sound, but in fact it is the way I personally experience the question for my own life. It seems to me that I must choose to be fully myself, to be a free Christian person. This means deciding to live fully with someone I love, in a role that is meaningful to me and trying in simple honesty to live out the faith for other Christians and for non-Christians. The alternative is to undertake the oppressive role of public loyalty to dogmas I don't accept, to work within a juridical Church framework which seems excessive and in many ways a re-establishment of Jewish law, to help keep going structures which are dying, and to try to insist with myself that a celibate life is still a reasonable option for me and does not entail the strong probability of a scandalous breakdown. I cannot see how this alternative will work. I will collapse morally, if not mentally, if I try to maintain such a role.

Father A., in fact, never posted this letter to his bishop. His second journey unfolded in its own way, and he still practices the priestly ministry in his own country. Despite the different ending, one sees how his case resembles that of Charles Davis: anger and resentment at "the official Church," and yearning for the chance "to live fully with someone whom I love."

Under the heading of "love and anger" belong many stories of husbands and wives who find themselves faced with infidelity or unexpectedly deserted by their spouses. Left to themselves, they would never have chosen the hard and bitter agony of such experiences. Resentment and frustrated affections can tear some of them apart. Yet others find within themselves the resources to cope and emerge—not consumed and wrecked by hatred, but possessing a strange wisdom that allows them to live with the complexities of good and evil. Eleanor Roosevelt is an outstanding example. The catalyst—or at least a notable cause—of her midpoint journey was the discovery that her husband had a mistress.

Mrs. B., the wife of a highly successful and popular executive, offers another example. They lived for twelve idyllic years in St. Louis. Then the company shifted her husband to California. When she followed some weeks later, she found her husband starting a pointless affair with a secretary nearly twenty years younger than himself. He had never been unfaithful before. Utterly confused and lost, Mrs. B. left to drive back to St.

Louis and wind up matters there. Unaware of what was happening, her two sons persuaded her to make a detour to see the Grand Canyon. "I looked down," she told me, "and wanted to throw myself over and end it all." Instead, she went back to St. Louis, took a job and experimented with affairs. She suffered a serious nervous breakdown and ran the whole gamut of subsequent treatments: therapies, drugs and analysis. Her husband Ted, even though he gave up his affair in its early stages and tried to heal the wounds by moving back East, was no longer a source of any consolation. She had had a glimpse of the ultimate when "no one is with me. No one can keep me safe." She had realized her life to be exactly the "stifling, static combination of mapped-out qualities and patterns of behavior," of which Bergman speaks. Putting things in the third person, she explained what had happened to her:

> The real drama for the Mrs. B. I know was not the fact of her husband's infidelity but the realization that her whole reason for being could be lost and unbelievably snatched away—that her reason for living was precarious and possibly worthless. The fact that you yourself refer to her not in her own right as "so and so" but as *Mrs.* B. is a proof in itself of what I am trying to say. This woman is no one, only a reflection of others, "mother of two," "wife of a highly successful and popular executive." Her life was centered entirely on that of her husband's—his job, his family, his home, his ambitions, even his friends. The journey West had meant the loss of her pleasant home and surroundings, the putting aside of familiar things and longstanding friendships. All this she did gladly, almost seizing the opportunity for a new start, a second honeymoon, unhampered by the trappings of a 12 year-old marriage. She was peculiarly ill-equipped to cope with the biggest loss of all—that of her husband. She had existed only as one of a pair.

But then she began to experience the paradox of a movement towards herself which would also bring her back to others. She took steps to learn to live with herself, a voyage of discovery undertaken in the knowledge and acceptance of the fact that Ted might not at all fancy staying with the person she now found herself to be. His "infidelity," perhaps an attempt at "freedom" for himself, thrust upon her the liberty to move towards herself and away from an injurious state of coupling where no expansion was tolerated and no growth was possible. "It's a weird experience," she observed, "to wake one day to find you have withered away or been eaten alive." She added:

> I must confess, despite the anger and hatred I suffered, I could not help from time to time having a twisted laugh at the fate that had dealt me such a load of wornout clichés! . . . It was in a way part of my salvation that even at the worst of times I could have a hysterical giggle . . . Humor plays a very large part in journeying, if one is to come out positively on the other side. I feel sure it is a sidekick to wisdom and if one can maintain a sense of humor, a sense of the ridiculous over some journeying manifestations, then maybe a little wisdom rubs off in the end.

Things grew better slowly. She started to feel sure that she would survive, even if Ted repeated his adventure or left altogether. She sensed that in time he would even be grateful that she would never again be "emotionally a total dependent." One experience proved peculiarly helpful.

> Last spring, while doing some very desultory gardening, I became aware of a curious feeling that I suspected might be the beginnings of peace. I did not try to examine the feeling too hard in case it promptly evaporated. I realized I was pruning the growth of ages from the plum trees. They could not have been touched in years, and as I pruned harder, I felt a self-confidence long since forgotten. I too had undergone a manic amputation but, given time and reasonable conditions, both the trees and I would show signs of growth. And so it was.

Marital infidelity may be the catalyst of a second journey. More broadly, it seems that *any* deeply disturbed relationship to some person or institution close to us can set off a second journey.

Dr. C. worked for seven years with a famous professor at a North American university. Success had come easily to Dr. C. The last years at high school were particularly happy. "We had a gentleman's agreement," he told me. "We studied hard at our specialties. Then we could play as much sport as we wanted. I left school very self-confident—in the spirit of 'Show me the world.'" With two friends he went to Europe on a kind of Grand Tour through Spain, Italy and Greece. College and graduate studies swept by happily and he found himself hired as an assistant professor by the man who had directed his research. Dr. C.'s first journey was over. It looked as if he had established himself and life would press on smoothly. If there were some obvious dangers, these were for others. "I knew," he commented, "how the boss cared for his students! This was only as long as their work contributed to his projects. He was a complete egoist. And every year or two he needed a human sacrifice."

The crash came when C.'s line of research no longer suited the head of the department. He found himself out of a job and, in fact, unlikely to get one if he stayed in his own country and his own field. He felt deeply angered and bewildered. A European university unwittingly came to the rescue by offering him a year's grant. C. took the trip and came home to North America with his bitterness gone, his equilibrium regained and a readiness to reckon with new commitments—even to abandon hopes of resuming his chosen area of academic life and enter politics. "When I lost my job," he recalled, "my mother said: 'You're at the age at which Christ was crucified.' It *was* painful then. But, strangely, I feel thankful now. We don't enjoy unlimited possibilities. Some things have to be accepted."


IV

SICKNESS


A crisis of love and anger in one's relationship toward a particular person or institution may set a second journey going.

However, something as seemingly prosaic as illness may turn out to be decisive in provoking and directing such a journey. The life of John Henry Newman (1801–90) exemplifies this.

In *Newman's Journey* (1974), the shorter version of her masterly two-volume biography, Meriol Trevor observes:

> Although childhood and adolescence form a human being, his mind and personality often take their individual set round about thirty, and this was so with Newman. He was just twenty-seven when Mary [his beloved sister] died and he became vicar of St. Mary's and he was thirty-two when he was brought near to death himself, by a fever in Sicily and came back to Oxford to begin the Movement of the Catholic revival.

Miss Trevor swings between journey and death-resurrection language in describing the trip which took Newman to the Mediterranean with some friends in 1833. "The whole of this journey was to be for Newman a voyage into his own soul, ending with a death and resurrection in Sicily." Newman himself mixed his images. After a first visit to Sicily, he went back there alone because he wanted to see what it would be like to be "solitary and a wanderer." He collapsed with a severe fever. Yet he was sure he would not die: "God has still a work for me to do." As he finally grew better, Newman felt he was enjoying "life from the dead." On his voyage home, he wrote the poem entitled "The Pillar of the Cloud," but which is generally known by its opening words.

> Lead, kindly Light, amid the encircling gloom,
>     Lead Thou me on!
> The night is dark, and I am far from home—
>     Lead Thou me on!
> Keep Thou my feet; I do not ask to see
> The distant scene—one step enough for me.
>
> I was not ever thus, nor prayed that Thou
>     Shouldst lead me on.
> I loved to choose and see my path; but now
>     Lead Thou me on!

I loved the garish day, and spite of fears,
Pride ruled my will: remember not past years.

So long Thy power hath blest me, sure it still
    Will lead me on
O'er moor and fen, o'er crag and torrent, till
    The night is gone;
And with the morn those angel faces smile
Which I have loved long since, and lost awhile.

Back in England, Newman found it "remarkable that a new and large sphere of action" opened up at once. Miss Trevor comments: "The fever burned up the past and released a tremendous spring of energy; Newman was going home possessed with the intuition that he 'had a work to do in England.' "

Much of what happened to Newman on that Mediterranean tour suggests a second journey: (1) the outer journey; (2) the loneliness; (3) the nearly fatal fever, which confronted him with his own emptiness, led to a self-discovery and set him free to work so energetically for others; (4) and—not least—the journey language which came so naturally to him in the poem he wrote on the trip home.

A war wound ended a military career and initiated a second journey for Ignatius of Loyola (? 1491–1556). His autobiography begins with 1521 and his injury in a battle at Pamplona. Ignatius was then twenty-nine or thirty years of age. The account covers the next seventeen years of his life—the travels, trials, studies and ministry that took him to Jerusalem, back to Spain, north to Paris, across the channel to England, back to Spain and then to his final home in Rome. John C. Olin remarks that "these years are the central years of Ignatius' life. They are the years . . . that open with his religious conversion and that witness his spiritual growth."[3] In fact, these are the years that make up the mid-point journey of one who throughout the autobiography calls himself "the pilgrim."

Three points call for attention in the story of Ignatius: the crises of emotions, the loneliness and the search for new goals.

His autobiography exemplifies the hollowness, longing, pain, desperation and other feelings that can people the mind during a second journey. Through the months of recovery from his wounds he experienced emotions of comfort and distress—"sad and happy thoughts," as he calls them. Learning to interpret and handle these fluctuating affections constituted a vital stage of his journey. The "Rules for the Discernment of Spirits" (found in his *Spiritual Exercises*) pass on to others what Ignatius first painfully found out for himself.

As a traveller on a second journey, Ignatius endured solitary trials—far from home, peace and company. His autobiography evokes the terror of one such occasion.

When he arrived at Genoa he took the road to Bologna, on which he suffered very much, especially one time when he lost his way and began to journey along a riverbank down below. The road was up above, but as he went farther along the path began to get narrower; and it became so narrow that he could no longer go forward nor turn back. He began to crawl along and in this way he covered a good distance with great fear, because each time he moved he thought he would fall into the river. This was the greatest toil and bodily travail that he had ever had, but at last he got out of it.

This story has a value that goes well beyond being merely an episode of fearful physical danger recalled by a saint in his old age. It symbolizes stunningly the condition of mind which can be suffered at some stages in the second journey. We can lose direction and be brought to our knees on an ever-narrowing path. High above us, others travel a seemingly safe road. But all we can do is crawl along in terror and loneliness. At every moment we risk falling into the water to drown alone. Like the ancient mariner we can feel ourselves

Alone, alone, all, all alone
Alone on a wide wide sea!

39

Lastly, Ignatius' midlife journey involved a crisis of goals and meaning. The journey's end loomed up only after long searching. The goal was neither seen nor even suspected at the outset. He was seventeen years on the road before he reached his destination. At times a sense of meaninglessness tortured the pilgrim. Ignatius recalls "the harsh thought" that deeply troubled him during the stay at Manresa. Had he chosen his own insane nightmare? Or was he following a God-inspired dream? Tormented by scruples, he even felt the temptation to take his own life.

## V

### WAR

It was an injury in action during battle that set Ignatius on a second journey. War itself may act as the catalyst—both in "real" life and in literature. The fall of Troy left Aeneas wandering for ten years before he settled in Italy to become the father of the Roman people. A military catastrophe drove the Trojan prince away from his settled place in society to face unexpected adventures and fulfill a strange destiny. Life did not prove one long plateau once Aeneas had grown to manhood and completed his first journey.

One of the most revered twentieth century martyrs, Dietrich Bonhoeffer (1906–45), offers a further example in which war was the decisive factor. Writers have made much of this German theologian's so-called conversion experience of 1931–32. He decided then to take the Sermon on the Mount as the pattern for his life. That phase, however, signalled the point of arrival, the end of Bonhoeffer's first journey. A later (crucial) turning-point in his life came in the summer of 1939 when he travelled to New York. He was trying to find a foothold in a tottering world.

Friends like Martin Niemöller were already held in concentration camps. The Nazi regime was working for the complete disintegration of the "Confessing Church," that association of Protestant Christians who, like Bonhoeffer, refused to compromise with Hitler's racism and other demonic policies. Bonhoeffer feared that he would soon be called up for military service. He drafted a will, left it with a friend and sailed for the United States.

American friends welcomed him warmly and flooded him with invitations to lecture at various colleges and universities or take a three-year post working for German refugees in New York City. Inwardly Bonhoeffer suffered deep anxiety. "The first lonely hours are difficult," he wrote in his diary. "I don't know why I am here." Even though he had often lived and travelled abroad, he was "terribly homesick." He felt thoroughly desperate and blamed himself for his "weakness" and "cowardice" in running away to New York. "The whole weight of self-reproach comes back and almost chokes one." "God," he prayed, "give me in the next week clarity about my future."[4]

What was he to do? The cruel inward conflict got mirrored in "Protestantism Without Reformation," the essay he began writing. "To hold out to the last," he reflected, "may be commanded, to flee may be allowed, perhaps even demanded. The Christian's flight in persecution does not of itself mean apostasy and disgrace, for God does not call everyone to martyrdom. Not fleeing but denial is sin."

At Union Theological Seminary, Bonhoeffer stayed in what the students called the "Prophets' Chamber." He fought out an interior battle pacing his room, walking the streets of New York and staying at the country home of the seminary's president. It finally seemed "unthinkable" to remain in the United States during the catastrophe that threatened to rip Germany apart. He wrote to Reinhold Niebuhr: "I must live through this difficult period of our national history with the Christian people of Germany. I will have no right to participate in the reconstruction of Christian life in Germany after the war if I do not share the trials of this time with my people." St. Paul's plea to Timothy echoed and re-echoed in his mind: "Do your best to come before the winter" (2 Timothy 4:21).

Bonhoeffer's American friends felt sharply disappointed when—a week after his arrival—he blurted out the news that he would not stay. Yet he himself was "not quite clear about the motives" for his decision. "Is that," he asked, "a sign of vagueness, of intellectual dishonesty, or a sign that we are led on beyond what we can discern?" On the evening of July 7, 1939, he sailed from New York. He noted in his diary: "Manhattan by night. The moon stands above the skyscrapers. It's very hot. *The journey is over*" (italics mine). He had been less than a month in the United States.

Bonhoeffer stopped ten days with his sister in London. There he learned that a colleague in Germany, Pastor Paul Schneider, had been tortured to death in Buchenwald. Bonhoeffer himself was arrested in 1943 and hanged in April 1945—just a few days before the war ended.

The smoke of debate drifts in layers over Bonhoeffer's life and letters. Hypotheses about this much-loved figure abound and have been frequently overhauled. Nevertheless, there is little point in fretting over possible challenges from the professionals in this field. The whole New York episode, with its attendant circumstances, has all the marks of a second journey: the turmoil of emotions, the loneliness as he faced his future, dissatisfaction with the solutions suggested by the American friends at hand and then the decision, at the age of thirty-three which settled forever the meaning of his life.

In the Roman legend, Aeneas fled from his defeated city to found a new people and a new empire. Bonhoeffer went back to his country on the eve of a military and moral catastrophe. In both stories, it was war which forced heroes to face the strange adventure of a midlife journey. The journey took Bonhoeffer home to his people—a movement that was also part of his final coming to himself.


## VI

### SOMETHING MORE?

In sorting out and grouping together second journeys, we have introduced some seemingly precise classifications like "exile" and "war." The differences are, of course, enormous between Aeneas, a mythical hero, and Bonhoeffer, the Christian martyr whose letters and papers from prison set post-war theological pulses racing. All the same, "war" counts as a sufficient resemblance to link together these two cases of a second journey.

Other midlife journeys can be grouped together on vaguer grounds. I have in mind those stories which match each other in exhibiting a yearning for "something more."

Mr. D. was a company director in his mid-forties. Concentration on business brought the usual rewards for a talented man: a large house in a wealthy suburb, two luxury cars and the rest. One day he found his mind freed from the fashion of accepting that "that's all there is." Was the toil really worth it? Would it be more valuable to give his wife more time and get to know his children? They were beginning to have the slightly robot look of having been made and not born. Mr. D. sold his property, bought a farm in the remote countryside, persuaded his family to give his plan the benefit of any qualms, and launched them all into life on the land. He wanted to try himself out again, this time doing "something more."

The decision to attempt "something more" has taken others in the opposite direction—from a small sphere of action out into the limelight. This is not their language. But Dr. E. and Mother Teresa of Calcutta belong here.

Dr. E. summed up her second journey this way: "I moved from a more structured thing to being out on my own." She had studied at two universities in a western country before helping to start a social institute. She stayed at that post for more than ten years. "I was deeply committed," she explained. "I tried to work harder than everyone else and got the job done." All those years she took what she called "the sublimation route." She was highly efficient, a "little bit dispassionate" and unwilling to "get out there and help in a way that risked being hurt."

At the age of thirty-eight she left the job—where she had been living "within good, safe structures"—and travelled to the United States to begin doctoral studies at an East Coast university. "I had to take a risk," she reflected, "even though what I chose was not accepted by some." She added: "It's not that I turned my back. I carried all those former years and past experiences with me. Where we have been illuminates where we are going."

In the United States, life with African, Asian and black

43

American students made her realize quickly that she came as a product of a racist culture. Some people warned Dr. E.: "If you mix with the blacks, the whites won't have anything to do with you." It was 1967. She knew she "had to make a leap—a qualitative leap in understanding." She faced the need "to understand people who from the beginning of their lives had suffered oppression." Two older people gave her emotional support during those early months in the United States. "They shared my humanity without sharing my new vision." The first semester ended. "After that I knew the road."

Dr. E. found herself marching for causes, working in Harlem and becoming associated with various radicals and revolutionaries. "If I mixed with startlingly different groups," she commented, "I remained conventional in behavior. What I had to do was really to accept people with very different life styles." She recalled the problem: "I came from a very respectable family, had lived within a protected structure and was now studying overseas on an esteemed scholarship." She accepted the possibility of not having her student visa renewed. Her thesis director warned her humorously: "I might have to bring the board to examine you a few yards across the Canadian border."

Looking back at those troubled years, she stressed the sense of vulnerability: "When you move out to help people, you *are* out in the open. You become vulnerable." Yet she refused to dramatize it all. "I was just one of many people working for civil rights. Of course, it was a risk. But it was the risk of having the lame, the halt and the blind in your house."

Without consciously identifying her experiences as a second journey, Dr. E. instinctively reached for the language of "the road." She quoted Robert Frost:

Two roads diverged in a wood, and I—
I took the one less travelled by,
And that has made all the difference.

She offered her own gloss. "The alternatives we face in life are extraordinary. It's like reaching a fork in the road. People warn you, 'Don't take that road.' You may think at first you are going ahead alone. But voices call you on. You can't ignore them."

Reflection on the road she had travelled in her late thirties and early forties let two conclusions emerge. (1) She had left her position as a helper who kept "some distance from others" in a "safe, professional career." Dr. E. found that roles were reversed. "Your vulnerability and struggles on the road allow other people to help you. It's when you fall on the road that the people you have tried to help on their journeys come to pick you up." (2) It was a shift that brought an encouraging sense of genuine community. "When I was a social worker," she mused, "I felt much more alone. I have come to feel surrounded by people. My feelings for others are much more intense now than when I was caught up with the need for physical comfort and sublimated that need into hard work."

The road Dr. E. took did not bring her to a fixed home. When she finished her doctorate, she decided against a "sure, well-travelled road" to a lively, new university in her own country and took a post instead at a university in a developing country. "I can't be absolutely sure," she admitted, "that I took the right road. There is no tenure in my journey. People say, 'Find yourself something else that is more secure.' "

Now forty-seven, Dr. E. told me: "My decision is to stay on until they say, 'We don't need you.' " "What's success then?" I asked. "Success," she replied, "comes when a person says, 'Don't hold my hand any more.' I hope my living has not been in vain. And yet—success or failure on our journeys doesn't really depend on the decisions *we* take."

She now sees the start of her second journey as motivated by the need for personal challenge and excitement—with "some idea of being a little bit different." She has found that "you have to pay a price for taking a less-travelled road," on which she cannot hope to enjoy the same sort of approval she had received on her earlier job. She quoted *One Flew Over the Cuckoo's Nest*: "The Big Nurse . . . knew that people, being like they are, sooner or later are going to draw back a ways from somebody who seems to be giving a little more than ordinary, from Santa Clauses and missionaries and men donating funds to worthy causes, and begin to wonder: What's in it for them?" Dr. E. hastened to add: "Some people draw back from you. But it's the other group—the people you meet on the road—that make the journey possible."

Mother Teresa of Calcutta (born 1910) provides another example of attempting "something more," one that has caught the world's imagination.[5] At the age of nineteen, she travelled out to India and began work in the Bengal Mission of the Loreto Sisters. Completing her first journey meant physically moving away from her "very happy" home in Yugoslavia to a new and self-chosen place on the far side of the world. She went through the stages others expected of her, taking her first vows two years later (in 1931) and then her final vows in 1937. She had settled down in what looked like a permanent role.

But nine years later she felt a "call within a call." "It was," she reflected, "a vocation to give up even Loreto where I was very happy and to go out in the streets to serve the poorest of the poor." Significantly, this experience took place *on a journey*—from Calcutta to the Himalayas. She recalled the day: "In 1946 I was going to Darjeeling, to make my retreat. It was in that train, I heard the call to give up all and follow him into the slums to serve him among the poorest of the poor." She applied for the necessary permissions to leave the convent and strike out on her own. Two years later all the official approvals had come through. Mother Teresa left the beautiful garden and "the quiet peaceful place" that had been her religious home. She walked out alone into the streets of Calcutta. Soon, however, she had fashioned a new and enduring community of sisters whose work for the dying, the utterly poor and the incurably ill inspires people round the world to share this kind of love in action.

Once again we have little trouble in spotting the features of a midlife journey. An inner voice heard on a long train-ride led a nun in her mid-thirties to discover the program for the second half of her life. This second journey let her work with tremendous energy to relieve human misery and do, as she put it, "something beautiful for God."

This chapter has searched out and grouped together various stories to illustrate what a second journey can look like. I wanted the contemporary cases to be as frank and factual as I could make them. More such cases could have been added.

46

Likewise, I could have piled up other names from history like Paul of Tarsus, Augustine of Hippo, Elizabeth Seton and Albert Schweitzer. But let us stand back to plot the patterns embodied in the stories and cases already given.

*Chapter Three*
*Mapping the Pattern*

We want, finally, a sense of things not ending but freshly beginning.

R.C. Hutchinson

It proves to be an illusion that everything can be reversed, that there is always time for everything and that everything somehow returns.

Hans Georg Gadamer

One reaction to my interpretation of Wesley, Dante, Eleanor Roosevelt, Newman, Ignatius of Loyola, Mother Teresa of Calcutta and others could be to say: "It's all very well. These are big names to play with. Even if I recognize something of a second journey in my life, I have no delusions about belonging in their company." Nevertheless, such great men and women do afford some larger context for interpreting the experience of lesser lives. Many people between thirty and sixty— whatever their stature or achievements—undergo what can truly be called a second journey. The big names can at least form a macrocosm for their microcosm.

Quite apart from the desire to decline any grandiose comparisons, one could also react to much of what has been said by remaining aloof and disengaged. The experience of Wesley and Carter, the poetry of Dante, the myth of Aeneas and other second journeys may prove interesting from an historical and literary point of view. The image of a second journey can pull together undoubted elements of human life and imagination. But does the reader recognize his or her own involvement in such a journey? How do Dante's *Inferno,* Wesley's *Journals* or Ignatius' autobiography match and illuminate the experience of today? The anonymous cases (Father A., Mrs. B., Dr. C., Mr. D., and Dr. E.) could help to bridge the gap. They give glimpses of what contemporary second journeys look like.

Mapping the characteristic pattern may also allow readers to relate to this image. A second journey is never found "neat." It is always embodied in particular lives, particular pieces of literature and particular myths. Yet, if we check through the material given in the last chapter and other cases, we find clear traces of a general pattern acted out in various lives and stories. It seems that at least six major features merit attention.

I

## "THRUST UPON THEM"

A second journey happens to people. They do not voluntarily enter upon it. Or, if they do willingly start it, they do not fully understand what this journey will mean for them. They can be swept into it by different factors. We can risk classifying all the stories into two classes, according to whether the "cause" is some observable phenomenon or is something "inward" and less publicly observable.[1]

The observable phenomenon may be something apparently positive, like being suddenly landed in a new and demanding job. Persons unexpectedly thrust into prominence can find themselves exposed and vulnerable. Or else the catalyst can be something obviously negative. A traffic accident, a serious illness, a war wound, the death or infidelity of a spouse can plunge people into unexpected crises. Left to themselves, they would never have chosen the pain of being a widow, a deserted wife, a paraplegic or a disabled war veteran. It all simply happened to them. The shooting on Bloody Sunday in Derry triggered off a second journey for Gail Sheehy. The battle of Pamplona and a long convalescence initiated a midlife journey for Ignatius. His severe illness caused his world and his vision of the world to disintegrate. Without his wanting or planning it, Ignatius suffered that profound upheaval which he records in his autobiography, and his second journey got under way. Many deliberate choices stud the later stages of his story. But the beginning of the pilgrimage was thrust upon him.

The catalyst can be something interior and less "physically" obvious. Some people may go away for a summer program, a sabbatical semester or long-service leave and abruptly find themselves hit by a sudden crisis that leaves them feeling confused and even lost. They cease to define themselves by their marriage, their career, their priesthood or their religious commitment. Their world has come apart at the seams. Present roles and obligations start looking absurd. Self-doubts and fears destroy their sense of settled coherence and leave them inwardly wandering in a state of suspended being—like ghosts from some unquiet grave. Or—to vary the image—they find themselves drowning in unfamiliar waters of turbulence and change. They would never have entered into such a state of their own accord.

A man can have piled up half a column of material for his national *Who's Who* and then wake up one morning thinking, "Is it all worth it?" He may feel abruptly compelled to change, to give up his profession and start all over again—perhaps at high financial cost and at an even higher cost to the stability of his family. Competent teachers, nurses and tradesmen can reach the top only to discover that the job no longer fascinates. There is nowhere higher to go. They find themselves terrified of stagnation and demanding: "Should I and can I switch careers? Would study at an open university help?"

Whether the causes which come into play are visibly apparent or less "tangible," one feature emerges clearly. Seemingly of their own volition, second journeys simply begin.

## II
### CRISES OF FEELINGS

We do not need to collect and diagnose many cases before observing that a second journey entails a crisis of affectivity. Such a crisis may concern primarily some current personal failure (Carter and Wesley), unresolved conflicts from the past (Jenny Isaksson) or fears for the future (Gail Sheehy). The last case offers a way in for reflection on this second feature of midlife journeys.

In fresh and compelling language, Gail Sheehy reports her

tumultuous feelings about the passage of time and the loss of youth. At the age of thirty-five she suddenly realized that life was running out. Death waited at the end of a shortening road. Her physical powers were beginning to slip. She glimpsed darkness at the end of the tunnel.

A crisis of feelings may cluster around the way one perceives time and the passage of time. Yet we would be misinterpreting this experience, if we viewed it as "nothing more than" a restlessness caused by the loss of youth. It would be a silly and dangerous form of reductionism to insist on approaching the phenomenon *merely* from that point of view. As we shall argue, there is much to said for Jung's notion that for people over thirty all problems are spiritual rather than psychological.

The past has a privileged place in the crises of feelings that shape and accompany second journeys. This seems especially true of those who have set themselves clear goals, repressed emotional reactions deemed unsuitable and pushed ahead relentlessly with the search for "success." Social workers can care for unmarried mothers, sisters can help to heal the sick and comfort the dying, doctors can work superbly for their patients, priests can absolve the guilty and minister splendidly to huge parishes. But all the time they may be protecting themselves from facing their own feelings. Public success can blind them to their own needs. These unwitting self-deceivers must eventually admit and cope with parts of themselves that got left out on their road to success. Deliberately chosen motivation and a resolute will can prove strong enough for years, until anger, hunger for affection and other suffocated emotions simply erupt from the depths of an outraged nature.

The heroine of *Face to Face*, Jenny Isaksson, has to let such suffocated feelings really break through for the first time. She must admit and grapple with aspects of her life which she had neglected. She finds nightmarish images rising up to confront her as she faces an agonizing self-reappraisal. She has spent her energy in being responsive to others. Now she feels forced to attend to herself. She has cared competently for her patients. She now experiences the compulsive need to care for herself. As Ms. Sheehy suggests, Jenny Isaksson and other

54

such experts with the answers for others need "time out" to become pilgrims with questions for themselves.

The emotional material that has been hoarded unheard can frequently concern our relationships with *people or institutions close to us*, as in Jenny's case. Hateful things done to her in childhood abruptly arose to torment her and throw her world into confusion. To face up finally to the cruelty, dishonesty or corruption of some persons or institutions can let deep anger burst through. Or else it may be a question of feeling unappreciated and unloved by the family, the spouse, the organization, the religious congregation or the diocese to which one has given one's life.

We could all select, arrange and describe several stories illustrating the crisis of affectivity which can develop around a person or institution close at hand. The case put by Charles Davis in *A Question of Conscience* will do to exemplify the point. His integrity became outraged by the corrupt ways he felt the Roman Catholic Church, an institution to which he had dedicated his life, continued to employ language and exercise its power. "Words," he believed, "were used not to communicate truth, but as a means of preserving authority without regard for truth. Words were manipulated as a means of power." He noted a similar degradation and debasement of language both in "papal encyclicals and documents from Roman Congregations," and "the pastoral letters of bishops" and "even many ordinary parochial sermons." "All reflect a similar corruption." His journey to Rome for the Vatican Council left him feeling "repelled" by "the methods used to assert and exercise papal power." Looking back at it all, he remarked: "I see now how twisted and inhibited my mind became in trying to conform, partly from a sincere desire to accept authority, partly from the pressure exerted by an authority prepared to suppress dissentients." The "climactic incident" in reaching his decision to quit the Catholic Church came in October 1966. A statement made by Pope Paul VI about birth control came across as "dishonest" and "a diplomatic lie." Charles Davis summed up his sense of outrage: "One who claims to be the moral leader of mankind should not tell lies."

Many of these points should be challenged. One cannot, for instance, overlook how exaggerated is the claim that "words were used not to communicate truth, but as a means of preserving authority without regard for truth." It would have been a very different case if Davis had maintained: "Words were used not only to communicate truth, but also as a means of preserving authority." Likewise, his description of the Catholic Church (which we cited earlier) as "a sea of unhappiness" is obviously extreme. It simply did not and does not match the experience of very many Catholics.

However, I do *not* wish here to argue for or against the credibility of the Roman Catholic Church or its head. The point to be drawn from the case of Charles Davis and others is simply this. Whatever particular way it goes, a powerful crisis of feelings always seems to blaze up as one is swept into a second journey.

Jung's reflections on middle life suggest what appears to hold true of most second journeys. The emotional shock centers on the past and the way one's life has gone so far.

Instead of looking forward one looks backward, most of the time involuntarily, and one begins to take stock, to see how one's life has developed up to this point. The real motivations are sought and real discoveries are made. The critical survey of himself and his fate enables a man to recognize his peculiarities. But these insights do not come to him easily; they are gained *only through the severest shocks* (italics mine) *Psychological Reflections*.

### III
### THE OUTER JOURNEY

Characteristically, a second journey includes an outer component—some specific journey or a physical restlessness that keeps one travelling in the hope: "If I relocate, I will find the solution."

The outer journey may prove a real *Odyssey* or *Aeneid*.

Nevertheless, such lengthy travels as a Ulysses or an Aeneas undertook are neither required nor sufficient. On the one hand, men and women who wander far afield in their middle years may turn out to be unchanged by their experiences.[2] Their wanderings need not become a genuine second journey. On the other hand, the outer journey may be only slight, just a few miles from one home to another. Some people seem to make their inner journey without its being instigated by or expressed in some notable outer journey. That outer journey may be no more than a shift from the suburbs to the city.

Wesley's voyage to Georgia, Bonhoeffer's second visit to New York, Newman's Mediterranean tour exemplify the longer movement through space which can bring a significant change of consciousness in the middle years. Ignatius' wanderings belong here: from Spain to the Holy Land, back to Spain, north for studies in Paris, back again to Spain and eventually journey's end in Rome. Jimmy Carter's mission to the northern states and Mother Teresa's 1946 train ride out of Calcutta typify less notable outward journeys which created contexts for interior journeys to take place.

Of course, it is the *inner* component which brings about a genuine second journey. The external travelling has only a subordinate function. All the same, some shift from place to place appears to be a steady feature of authentic midlife journeys.

Nothing catches better the link between the outer and inner journeys than a letter written to me by a priest. He passed through a midlife journey which saw him shift restlessly from place to place. With his permission I quote a key passage:

During the late sixties and into the seventies I often felt filled with an aching hollowness, wanting to escape loneliness and find someone to share my daily life with. It was an unspecified longing, not a desire to marry some particular woman or to search belatedly for my girl friend of college days. One day I stood transfixed as I glimpsed a poster carrying Thoreau's observation, "The mass of men lead lives of quiet desperation." That described my state. It reinforced a judgment on my restlessness which persistently rose to the surface of my mind: "An organism in pain keeps moving."

## IV
### MEANING, VALUES AND GOALS

The afternoon of life, according to Jung, brings "the *reversal* of *all* the ideals and values that were cherished in the morning" (italics mine). These are strong words. Gail Sheehy is content to speak simply of facing "the spiritual dilemma of having no absolute answers." Whether we press the point strongly or make it more gently, second journeys bring a search for new meaning, fresh values and different goals.

Very many people choose external goals to define their existence. They aim at becoming head of their department in the public service, a bishop in a large diocese, secretary to their trade union, principal of a high school, a journalist for a leading newspaper or some other "top" person. They move upward in society and then one of two things may happen to them in their thirties, forties or fifties: (1) they reach their goal and it bores them, or (2) they realize that they may never attain it and panic sets in.

If the first thing occurs, then the roles by which they identified themselves no longer seem important. The old purposes fade. The values and goals which gave meaning to life lose their grip. The second alternative fits stories like those of Jimmy Carter, John Wesley and Ignatius of Loyola. It was, as Carter admitted, a "very difficult time" for him in 1966, when he lost so narrowly the Democratic primary election for the Georgia governorship. Wesley set his heart on being a dedicated and successful missionary. But his dream shattered and after two years in Georgia he had to return to England. The wound Ignatius suffered during the battle at Pamplona healed but left some bone sticking out in an ugly fashion. He was so anxious to retain his role as an elegant officer that he persuaded the surgeons to cut away the protruding piece of bone. Without a murmur, he endured the primitive surgery—driven on by the fear that he would lose an identity by which he had defined his existence. But then his second journey led him to find other values, new goals and a different identity.

In one way or another persons on a second journey want "more" out of life. Questions come flooding at them: "What have I done? Has my life been productive or stagnant? Would it be worth doing it all over again? What is the 'more' I want?" Charles Davis and Father A. talked about "rebuilding" their lives. Mr. D. wanted to try himself out again. That involved clarifying fresh values by which to shape some new commitments. In his mid-thirties, Paul Gauguin gave up a "good" job as a banker, left his wife, launched himself into a second life as a painter and settled in the South Seas. A painting he did at the age of forty-nine shows attractive people and a pleasant panorama, but carries these words in lieu of a title: "Where did we come from? What are we? Where are we going to?" These are questions that a second journey typically throws up.

The answers may turn up fairly quickly. A year or so after his painful defeat, Carter went through his born-again experience. Wesley sailed back across the Atlantic—a deeply troubled man. Only a few months later, he felt his heart "strangely warmed" at a meeting in London, and found new and decisive purposes. The way ahead became clear. Fresh goals and satisfying meaning may, however, take time to appear. The second journey's end may loom up only after long searching and patient waiting. We return to this theme in the next chapter.

# V
## LONELINESS

People on second journeys repeatedly betray a deep sense of loneliness. This loneliness should eventually turn into the aloneness of a quiet and integrated self-possession. But before that happens, they will find themselves in Dante's "dark wood." In *Passages*, Gail Sheehy put her sense of loneliness this way: "A powerful idea took hold: *No one is with me. No one can keep*

*me safe. There is no one who won't ever leave me alone.*"
Coupled with this loneliness can also be the feeling of breaking
new ground, of travelling in a strange direction with no models
on the road just ahead. A second journey can encourage the
sense of being without a guide and being like an Abraham called
forth from one's accepted place in society to undertake odd
adventures. In *A Question of Conscience*, Charles Davis makes
no secret about sensing that he had been driven to do something
almost unheard of—a leading theologian walking out of the
Roman Catholic Church.

In her distress Ms. Sheehy called for help from one individual, her boyfriend in New York. But he left her disappointed
and she sprang to the conclusion: "Each of us travels alone. No
one else can always keep us safe."

In many cases, it is a group of people or society in general
that creates and sustains the sense of loneliness. Someone who
ventures beyond the bounds of the group consensus or shows
clear dissatisfaction with the community ideals can hardly expect anything else. The suburban wife who abruptly finds that
ordinary values and goals no longer work will appreciate the
lonely frustration of one woman on a second journey who told
me: "My friends never know what I am talking about." A sister
realizes she cannot keep playing her accustomed role. Her
congregation will want to know, "Why can't she stick at the
good work she's doing?" A doctor or a priest on a second
journey may seem to have zigzagged off the normal course.
Medical colleagues and diocesan authorities will demand:
"What the hell does he think he's doing? He's chasing self-
fulfillment—in his own way and on his own terms." Anyone
who does not match society's expectations will hardly find
much support from others.

Eventually, the person who has passed through a midlife
journey may transform the consciousness of his or her community. Many of the people discussed in chapter two finally prodded their societies into attaining higher viewpoints and accepting more generous commitments. The hero or heroine of a
second journey may even resemble Aeneas in fashioning a
whole new community. However, much loneliness, some deep
suffering at the hands of society, or even, as in the case of

Bonhoeffer, death, may have to intervene before the individual reshapes in one way or another his world.


## VI
### WISDOM AND POWER

The sixth and last feature in the pattern of second journeys touches the journey's end. Ideally, such journeys end *quietly*, with a new *wisdom* and a coming to oneself that releases great *power*. Even if we do not attach equal weight to each of these themes, they deserve to be developed.

Second journeys typically begin dramatically: parachutists shooting people (Gail Sheehy), a traffic accident, a public scandal, a cannon ball sweeping over the ramparts (Ignatius), the loss of an apparently secure job (Dr. C.), the discovery of a spouse's infidelity (Mrs. B.), a close election defeat (Carter), or a severe illness when travelling alone (Newman). The ending tends to be quiet and undramatic. Ignatius limps into Rome seventeen years later. One spring morning Mrs. B. finds "the beginnings of peace." Dr. C. comes home feeling that "some things have to be accepted." Midlife journeys close so quietly that—in nearly all the cases I have cited—one cannot be too positive exactly *when* journey's end occurred.

Second journeys terminate with the arrival of the new wisdom of a true adult.[3] It is a wisdom of one who has regained equilibrium, stabilized and found fresh purposes and new dreams. It is a wisdom that gives some things up, lets some things die and accepts human limitations. It is a wisdom that agrees, "I cannot expect anyone to understand me fully." It is a wisdom that has learned through suffering to live with human finitude and admit the inevitability of old age and death.

This wisdom accepts the mystery of the world's evil and good and—without collapsing into compromise—attains a final integrity by which to live. Such a wisdom has faced the pain caused by parents, colleagues or superiors, truly forgiven them, and acknowledged with an unexpected tenderness that these people are neither angels nor devils but only human.

This mature wisdom is another name for coming to oneself

in an ultimate self-discovery and a final self-identification. One has found a new center, an integrating factor that has been lifted to consciousness and conceptualized. All this means building on one's past, integrating one's present experience with what has happened and achieving a sense of definitive selfhood for the future.

This new wisdom involves self-discovery but not self-seeking. Those who have found a new center and an integrating factor have now a confident message to deliver. They demonstrate the paradox of a movement towards themselves which has brought them back to others. These solitaries who have achieved peace can reach out to others and prove astonishingly productive for the world. Their second journeys end with new dreams in which fresh responsibilities begin. For the benefit of others they live out what they have experienced for themselves. They share the conviction of Newman who heads home, sensing that he has "a work to do in England."

All that has just been said about wisdom, power and self-discovery risks being talk about the *ideal* order. The stories given above concern people who have made more or less successful second journeys. At any rate, *no clear cases* have been cited of journeys that have aborted or obviously failed. All turns out well in the ideal stories. But for many travellers on a second journey, the sixth point may *not* be nearly as true to the degree that the other five are. A genuine journey's end need never occur or may fail to bring a final resolution of the issues. It is not that such travellers are ultimate failures and ruined forever. But a true and powerful integrity may simply not come. The sixth point could state matters in too positive terms. It seems demonstrably mistaken to ignore the ragged and unfinished quality of many human lives.

For the most part, this chapter has struggled with the phenomena of successful second journeys and attempted to sketch the characteristic pattern. What suggestions emerge for those who can identify themselves with what has been stated but feel a deep ambiguity in their lives? What pieces of advice can be drawn from what has been argued so far? To these questions we now turn.

*Chapter Four*
*Coping with Second Journeys*

A person in the second half of life . . . no longer needs to educate his conscious will, but . . . to understand the meaning of his individual life, needs to experience his own inner being.

C. G. Jung

The dragon sits by the side of the road, watching those who pass. Beware lest he devour you. We go to the Father of Souls, but it is necessary to pass by the dragon.

St. Cyril of Jerusalem

In *Dry Salvages,* T. S. Eliot writes: "We had the experience but missed the meaning." Experiences become different when identified. Profound experiences that are neither described nor even named can turn terrifying. This holds true of second journeys. Sheer acknowledgment may, just by itself, release some pilgrims from excessive fears and anxieties.

For those who undergo a second journey it can bring relief to be freed from the temptation to misinterpret their experience as "nothing more than" some odd bout of restlessness provoked by the loss of youth. The image of the second journey is there to explain and guide their self-exploration. It lets them come alive to the full range and scope of what is happening.

Of course, the image will neither totally dissolve the pain nor solve all the questions. But the account it offers can make a vital difference. Jung's reflections on the process of individuation seem apropos.

It is the task of the conscious mind to understand these hints. If this does not happen, the process of individuation will nevertheless continue. The only difference is that we become its victims and are dragged along by fate towards that inescapable goal which we might have reached walking upright, if only we had taken the trouble and been patient enough to understand the meaning of the numina that cross our path (*Psychological Reflections*).

In just that way the image of a second journey allows us to become participants in, rather than victims of, what we experience.

Granted that the whole attempt to isolate and identify second journey phenomena rings true, what suggestions result for those who recognize such phenomena in their present or past experiences? Four particular pieces of advice seem called for.


I

ACCEPTANCE

A second journey needs to be accepted for its spiritual and human possibilities. This is easier said than done. Such a journey—to echo St. John's Gospel—means being "carried where we do not wish to go" (21:18). I wonder how many second journeys have been aborted either by the various institutions to which people belong or by the individuals themselves. We can try to dismiss the onset of such a journey as little more than an unpleasant interlude. At best, it will simply go away of its own accord. At worst, it can be contained.

We can deny what is happening to us, take refuge in compulsive activity and resort to some coping techniques that satisfactorily handled crises in the past. Someone who was called to a second journey described to me his initial efforts to fend it off: "I worked harder and drank too much. I kept resisting but finally the pain overwhelmed me. And I let it happen." He fled the issues. But, ultimately, he had to take them in hand. Another person put it this way: "Eventually I had to let the 'breakdown' occur, and it became in fact the 'shakeup.' "

Fear, or at least caution, suggests resorting to placebos. A second journey looks like a risky thing. "If you haven't made it by forty, you will never make it." Letting go is not what people normally feel like doing in that situation. Mostly, they prefer not to leave go of nurse, "for fear of meeting something worse."

Yet to open ourselves to a second journey will let it re-enact itself in our individual lives. We must let go if we are to be broken up, remade and restructured. Our world suddenly comes apart at the seams. We cannot mend it. Let it come apart—even at the cost of much pain.

To vary the image—second journey people must die to be reborn. The rebirth can be harder than any birth. Martin Luther delighted in this eighth-century antiphon: "Media vita in morte sumus (in the middle of life we are in death)." The antiphon hints at that profound dying to which we may be called in our middle years.

In *Face to Face*, Jenny Isaksson remarks: "If you force everything to be as usual, then it *will* be as usual." A second journey threatens to modify life in a painful way. Can we bear to do so? Or will we revert to "tried and true" methods for containing the situation and forcing everything to be as usual?

In Greek mythology, Ulysses initially refused to honor the oath requiring him to help Menelaus recover his wife. When Palamedes arrived at Ithaca, Ulysses feigned madness in order to escape from his obligation. But Palamedes discovered that he was shamming and persuaded him to join the expedition to Troy. This myth is profoundly right. It reflects the instinctive response of men and women summoned in midlife to leave their settled places and walk strange roads, as well as their need to capitulate. Final acceptance and not damaging resistance is the order of the day for those called forth on an *Odyssey* in their middle years. For them a second journey is not a therapeutic option, but a prerequisite for genuine survival.

## II
### COUNTERFEIT DESTINATIONS?

The advice to let second journeys happen is not intended to encourage readers to abandon commitments recklessly and let themselves be swept away towards false goals. This advice does not mean lending cheap approval to those who cut and run in the spirit of "It's time to get out from under the wraps. It's time to 'do my thing.' " There exists a clear danger of settling for some counterfeit destination rather than moving towards that true journey's end to which the traveller is called. Hollow meaninglessness and aching loneliness can be profoundly troubling. One wonders how many pilgrims trustingly begin second journeys, but in their bewilderment end by taking some escape route along the way.

Such inauthentic solutions can occur in three ways. First, a counterfeit destination could take the form of cutting the journey short. It may take five or ten years, or even longer, before the goal of the second journey swings into view. Nature and society arrange much of the timing for a *first* journey. Puberty arrives on schedule; schooling ends. In some cultures marriage still takes place with statistical regularity within the space of a few years. The progress and pace of the first journey can be largely out of our control. But we can affect the length and duration of a second journey, even if its onset is thrust upon us. Years of patient travelling may be needed before the goal of our midlife journey shows up and that profound process of self-perception enters on its final lap. Only then will vague suspicions give way to positive discovery. The sense of inner stalemate and hurt will drain away. Strength and comfort will arise from finally seeing the meaning of what we have painfully experienced. But it may take much time and patience to pass through all the frustration, inner tensions and confusions to that final self-identification.

One man on a second journey expressed it this way: "I simply have to tough it out." A wife reflected on the risk of impatiently cutting the journey short: "This is particularly so for women who, after the child-bearing and rearing days are over, find a glaringly obvious void left and are tempted into rushing into a career to forestall the real identity crisis." T. S. Eliot's words in *East Coker* suggest the need for patience:

In order to arrive there . . .
You must go by a way wherein there is no ecstasy.

As Northrop Frye remarks in *The Secular Literature* (1976), "the happy endings of life, as of literature, exist only for survivors."

Even if we respect the proper timing of our second journey, we may literally *choose* the wrong goal. That is the second shape an inauthentic solution could assume. It might mean something extreme like the suicide to which Ignatius of Loyola and Mrs. B. felt drawn when they struggled with their midlife journeys. It might mean attempting to disappear and begin afresh in another part of the world—the "leaving-our-clothes-on-the-beach" solution. More often, such inauthentic solutions entail publicly abandoning serious commitments with which in fact we should stick. Either way, we refuse to face and resolve the painful issues that set our second journey going. We simply run away and clutch at something else—crying out, "I can't take it any more."

Here, of course, we may find ourselves extremely puzzled. False choices can occur when we do real harm to others. But can we know that *this* choice will mean damaging people in an unacceptable way and is not simply failing to meet their expectations?

Like forged cheques, a counterfeit destination can look like the real thing. Pilgrims need prudence to find their way through. Ignatius of Loyola's "Rules for the Discernment of Spirits" aimed to help Christians cope with just that—picking their way through a turmoil of feelings and a play of motivations to find the true choice and the genuine destination. Nothing less than a steady willingness to be enlightened by God's Spirit can safeguard their choice.

A third way midlife journeys go astray is by *regress*. Pilgrims on such journeys do not know where they are headed or how to interpret fully their present experience. They may be tempted to look back for something in which they can believe completely and which will give their lives the sharp focus of generous dedication. Underneath all this can lie a forlorn quest for lost innocence, a yearning to make one's way back to some naive commitment in a much simpler world where everything would be perfectly clear. The title of Thomas Wolfe's novel *You*

*Can't Go Home Again* warns the pilgrim to press forward trust-ingly towards a new future and not to attempt any false return to a past that is no more. The original experience of wholeness cannot be recovered just as it was.

Donald Howard and Reinhold Röhricht have drawn atten-tion to a feature of medieval literature about pilgrimages to Jerusalem. Of the 526 accounts they examined, none depicted a return. This pilgrimage, and all the more the pilgrimage of life, was understood as a one-way journey. No tales are told by Chaucer's pilgrims on the way back from Canterbury. Yet, is it true that second journeys are always one-way journeys?

### III
#### JOURNEY'S END

Second journeys may end in two ways. (1) The pilgrims reach a new place and a fresh commitment (Mother Teresa, John Wesley, Newman, Dr. E. etc.); (2) Or else they return to their original place and commitment, *only to reaffirm them in a new way* (Jenny Isaksson, Mrs. B., etc.). In brief, the journey's end shows whether we have been dealing with an *Aeneid* or an *Odyssey*.[1]

After the city of Troy is destroyed, Aeneas struggles, sur-vives and finally arrives at a distant land to fulfill his unexpected destiny as founder of the Roman people. Ulysses sets off for home from the same war. But he is swept along into an exciting series of adventures. He finally comes back to his wife, his son and his kingdom. T. S. Eliot's words in *Little Gidding* fit this second possibility:

We shall not cease from exploration
And the end of all our exploring
Will be to arrive where we started
And know the place for the first time.

In a sense, *all* second journeys are one-way journeys. A genuine *Odyssey* is no regress, no mere circular movement

70

where the conclusion simply restates the theme of the opening. The pilgrim may return to the same house, the same job and the same spouse but with a wisdom and understanding that now knows them all "for the first time."

Here, of course, the pilgrim faces the unnerving alternative. Is *my* second journey meant to be an *Aeneid* or an *Odyssey*? Does my journey summon me to explore and accept in a fresh way some lifelong dedication which I have already made? Or does it call me to give up some long-term commitment and reverse a deep decision which I had thought to be irrevocable?

The midlife journey for a married person might end with separation or divorce. Or it could create the new conditions for an intensified married life with the present partner. And that is a very different thing from merely sticking it out in the resigned mood of "We stayed together just because of the children."

"The dragon," Cyril of Jerusalem warns us, "sits by the side of the road." One thing which will allow us to continue along the road, pass by the dragon and come to the true journey's end is prayer.


## IV
### PRAYER

Gail Sheehy observes, "Each of us travels alone. No one else can always keep us safe." For the believing traveller, however, and perhaps even for the half-believer, prayer can deal with a felt loneliness and provide a strengthening assurance. Iris Murdoch remarks in *The Sovereignty of the Good*: "Whatever one thinks of its theological context, it does seem that prayer can actually induce a better quality of consciousness and provide an energy for good action which would not otherwise be available."[2] In his solitude, Newman cherished prayer and left behind the classic prayer for a second journey:

Lead, kindly Light, amid the encircling gloom,
    Lead Thou me on!
The night is dark, and I am far from home—
    Lead Thou me on!

71

Those persons whose lives have been consciously touched by God will not really or readily come to journey's end without prayer. Only that can turn such persons from being mere vagrants into becoming genuine pilgrims. Nothing less than the deep experience of God can ensure that their second journey will lead somewhere in the end. It takes faithful praying to transform incoherent wanderings into a genuine midlife journey. In their own odd way the *Aeneid* and the *Odyssey* make this point. Deities are always lurking around to help the heroes on their way. Aeneas and Ulysses are aware of their need for such supernatural help if they are to survive.

This is not to deny just how hard and even unpleasant persistence in prayer can be. Yet nothing less than faithful praying can transform restless tramps into true pilgrims. It always appears to me mildly amazing whenever people try to understand their lives at depth without recourse to prayer. If Dante gave us the classic statement of the second journey, we forget at our peril how prayer and the spirit of prayer pervade the *Divine Comedy*.

Such then are the four pieces of advice that could help people to cope with a second journey. (1) Accept it for its spiritual and human possibilities; (2) beware of counterfeit destinations; (3) remember that journey's end may either bring you to a new place in society or else result in a new way of facing some existing commitment; (4) keep more than the rumor of prayer alive if you are to "pass by the dragon" which sits by the side of the road.

*Chapter Five*
*Travelling with the Tiger*

All of man's contacts with grace or revelation, if they do not inevitably originate in symbol, end there.

T. F. O'Meara

The success of this book, if it has any success, will be to lead readers to very specific insights about their lives. The image of the second journey may assist some to reimagine their lives as wholes when other images and symbols seem broken and powerless.

Rereading the manuscript suggests adding two things: first, a set of quick warnings, and then, some material for a particular class of readers, men and women who live religiously dedicated lives.

## I

The warnings touch the danger of absolutizing the second journey and the elements that make it up. Such an absolutizing tendency could show itself in various ways. We might falsely argue that *everyone* must face a second journey. That would mean ignoring what we might call the "smooth evolvers," the many people who assume each phase of life and build on it without much fuss or bother. Many lives reveal such a smooth process of growth.

We could also get things wrong by supposing that every second journey will show up clearly *all* the characteristics we have noted. It would be fallacious to set down a detailed pattern to which all second journeys were supposed to conform precisely. Family resemblances rather than exact correspondences emerge from the cases reviewed in chapter two.

Further, readers need to be cautioned against absolutizing the *differences* between a second journey and the first and third journeys. All three journeys resemble each other in that they throw up a whole range of psychic, intrapersonal and social issues which must be dealt with. These are the issues within myself, those which concern an immediate circle (of relatives and/or other people) and those which concern society. All of life's journeys entail coping, albeit in different and distinct ways, with these three sets of issues. Further, as Dr. E. reminded us, we cannot simply turn our backs on the past. We always carry with us parts of the earlier stages of our lives. There can be no absolute difference between the first, second and third journeys.

Finally, in certain cases there may not be a clear separation between these journeys. Some people may never complete their first journey and reach a psychological integration—even provisionally. Almost without a break, these people move into a second journey simply because their first journey left their problems quite unresolved. (St. Augustine could well be a case in point.) Likewise, a second journey may have no end—neither a genuine journey's end nor even a counterfeit destination. Some people can simply fail to resolve the issues thrown up by their midlife journey. They make the third journey towards death without having reached an ultimate integration.


II


In the preface, I stated my reasons for not addressing this little book simply to one specific audience—those men and women who follow a life of religious dedication. The second journeys of such people can match (surprisingly?) those of others. To agree that this parallelism is truly "surprising" would let some false theological suppositions filter through. Dedication to a religious way of life does not mean a departure to some transcendental realm beyond the "ordinary" conditions of human existence. By calling some few people in this way, God neither disengages them from the general phenomena that affect the lives of other men and women, nor—specifically—exempts them from the possible challenge of a second journey. A religiously dedicated life does not automatically bring a miraculous change. God's invitation works within the parameters of genuinely human possibilities, not beyond them. In observing the phenomena of a second journey, we are contemplating something fundamental about the sources and directions of human life as such.

That said, we can afford to add some specific reflections on the second journey and religiously dedicated life.

First things first. The reactions from those who read my piece in the *Review for Religious* (May 1976) convinced me more than ever of a painful lacuna. So much "spirituality" is written for the young, for people still completing their *first* journey. One thinks of Rodriguez (*The Practice of Perfection and Christian Virtues*), Tanquerey and other writers. Rodriguez's volumes came from his conferences for Jesuit novices. Other standard works on the spiritual and religious life were likewise addressed to beginners: the young sister or brother, the seminarian and the newly-ordained priest or minister. The primary audience was intended to be people moving through their late teens on into their late twenties. A few classics on mysticism aimed to help older people, but looked explicitly only at the area of prayer. By and large it is depressing to see how rarely spiritual writers thought of taking up the *specific* needs of men and women on a second journey or, for that matter, on their third journey.

The tiny amount of writing I have come across that deals with mature men and women usually carries a title like *Weariness in Well-Doing*. The supposition comes through loud and clear. Virtuous resolutions made in the novitiate or training college can dribble away. Serious programs for progress drawn up by the young man or woman can corrupt easily. There will be compromises brought by trying to do good over a long period of time. But all of this is presumed to be just the wear and tear of human living. Religiously dedicated people should strive to

77

persevere—unchangingly—in that "state of perfection" to which they have committed themselves. Such spirituality assumes that "good" religious life, after the initial periods of training, is a long plateau on which one should endeavor to stay. For centuries the standard spirituality has hoped to communicate *a received body of truth* which should be applied throughout a consecrated life. This was to forget that truth is a dynamic growth-process. Fresh terminology could help here to preclude fallacies. Why not speak of religious life as a "*process of perfection*"?

Just occasionally, writers on the spiritual life have recognized that there could be a "second conversion" which occurs fifteen or twenty years after one's first conversion or commitment to religious life. This theme kept alive the rumor that after some years of dedication events might take a strikingly new turn. Talk of second conversion allowed for a deep movement of self-discovery in the middle years—a process which is better identified as a second journey.

All in all, however, spirituality took its focus and standards from the experiences and struggles of those on the first journey. Religious men and women have been expected to keep measuring themselves on that scale. Too often they believed themselves wanting, whereas in fact what they needed was a second journey perspective by which to raise and settle questions about themselves. A paraphrase of Jung's remarks (quoted in the preface) disconcertingly, if with some exaggeration, suggests the predicament of many religious in their middle years.

Wholly unprepared, they embark upon the second half of life. Or are there perhaps novitiates for forty-year-old religious people which prepare them for their coming life and its demands as the ordinary training programmes introduce our young people to a knowledge of religious life? No, thoroughly unprepared religious men and women take the step into the afternoon of life; worse still, they take this step with the false assumption that their truths and ideals will serve them as hitherto. But they cannot live the afternoon of religious life according to the programme of that life's morning: for what was great in the morning will be little at evening, and what in the morning of religious life was true will at evening have become a lie.

Of course, this is too strong as it stands. Some values *are* permanent, even though they may need to be purified, drastically reinterpreted and seen more maturely. It would be absurd to dismiss as "a lie" what had been true "in the morning of religious life." Nevertheless, one can sense the real point of such a Jungian exaggeration. There is need for a spirituality shaped for "the afternoon of religious life."

It is one thing to observe the lack of second journey spirituality. It is quite another to develop such a spirituality in detail. Here let me at least offer three reflections which may help to lay the ground for such a project. Chapter three traced six features which form the pattern of second journey stories. All of these bear application to religious life. Here I want to make three comments which could help Roman Catholics (and perhaps others) who lead religiously dedicated lives.

Second journeys, I argued, are thrust upon people. They simply begin—seemingly of their own volition. This quality of "happening to people" says something about a vital shift in spiritual attitudes that a second journey involves. First journey spirituality—both its theory and practice—typically highlights the generosity of youth. In chapter two we noted the detailed and heroic program to which the young Wesley gave himself. This is the spirituality which actively goes looking for the Lord (John 1: 37ff.). At best, it unselfishly volunteers in the spirit of "I will go. I will do it." At worst, this first journey spirituality deteriorates into a do-it-yourself holiness, which gives human efforts a primacy over the initiatives of divine grace.

The second journey, however, means being called forth to walk strange roads, experiencing massive disruptions and facing the pain of a rebirth. In short, a second journey invites one primarily to *acceptance* rather than *activity*.

Peter's question in John's Gospel serves as a motto for first journey spirituality: "Lord, to whom shall we go?" (6:68). But then Peter must be broken up and remade through the events of the passion and crucifixion. Reshaped by a kind of second journey, he becomes ready to accept a world in which he will be "'carried" where "he does not wish to go" (21:18). It is a vital change: from "going" to being willing to be "carried."

Chapter three named a search for new meaning, fresh values and different goals as a feature of second journeys. Quite a few religious men and women seem to nurse themselves through such crises of goals and meaning by clinging to some text or commonplace: "It's better to be part of the solution rather than part of the problem"; "Love is the revenge of noble souls"; "The glory of God is man fully alive"; "The only consolation is to love." Often such phrases and slogans are employed without much criticism. But they do help those religious who feel lost to grope toward interpreting their present existence and find meaning. Such favourite sayings can ease the sense of quiet desperation.

Finally, religious on a second journey want "more" out of life. Yet, what is the "more" they want? Chapter three recalled the way Gauguin put his second journey questions: "Where did we come from? What are we? Where are we going to?" Here, as elsewhere, getting the questions right may prove to be more important than clearly finding the true answers. Religious men and women cannot be satisfied with such a self-regarding way of putting the questions. Their questions must be phrased in terms of Christ. Like Gauguin, Ignatius of Loyola looked at past, present and future, but his second journey questions took this form: "What have I done for Christ? What am I doing for Christ? What ought I to do for Christ?" Religious on a midlife journey will scrutinize the values and goals by which they have identified themselves. But this search, if it is to be truly Christian, can only take place with and through Christ.

The "second journey" is an image of human self-definition which can make sense of one's middle years. But this image will be enormously enriched if viewed in the light of him whose dying allows one to be remade in the fullness of life.

### III

For most of this book, I have tried to address a general audience of readers—people who interpret their lives at depth but who need not be Christians or at least practicing Christians. Such an audience, if they have continued reading thus far, will surely let me express my own faith in these closing pages. Repeatedly the material made me want to speak of Jesus Christ. Take Jung's conviction that for people over thirty all problems are spiritual rather than psychological. This can be made more specific. For Christians over thirty all problems are Christological rather than psychological. For them, the ultimate self-discovery arrives when they find a new center—in Christ. Here is the integrating factor that brings mature wisdom and true productivity for their world.

In the New Testament, nothing suggests more beautifully Christ's place in a midlife journey than Luke's story of the road to Emmaus (24:13-35). Before the crucifixion the two disciples had gone to follow Jesus. Now—on a kind of second journey—they found the horror of his death thrust upon them. In a state of emotional shock they were clearing out—to rethink their values, seek fresh goals and risk settling for some counterfeit destination. But then they rediscovered Jesus, or rather were rediscovered by him, the stranger who fell into step beside them on their lonely road. That experience gave them a new equilibrium and sent them back to Jerusalem, ready to readjust their lives in the light of an unexpected and impossible dream.

There seems no better way of ending this book than by quoting a sermon I published in the *Clergy Review* for April 1976.[1] That piece on "Christ the Tiger," although it failed to use second journey terminology, in fact said what I wish to end with here. Christians on a second journey always travel with Christ, even if they are not conscious of that "stranger" with them. By sensing his presence they will definitively identify themselves.

A nineteenth century Hindu mystic, Ramakrishnan, once told a story about an orphaned tiger-cub. This tiger-cub, whose mother had been killed by hunters, was found by a herd of goats and raised with their young to believe that he too was a goat. One day the goats were out in the jungle, grazing in a clearing, when in stalked a great king-tiger. His fierce roar terrified the goats who ran off into the surrounding jungle. Suddenly, the tiger-cub, who thought he was a goat, found himself all alone in the presence of the king-tiger.

At first, the tiger-cub was afraid and could only bleat and sniff in the green grass. But then he discovered that, although he was afraid, yet he was not afraid—at least not like the others who had run off to hide. The king-tiger looked at the cub and let out a great roar. But all the cub could do in response was to bleat and gambol in the grass. The great tiger, realizing then that the cub imagined himself to be a goat, took him by the scruff of the neck and carried him to a pond. On the clear surface of the pond the cub would be able to see that he was like the great tiger. But all the cub did, when he saw their images mirrored side by side, was to bleat, goatwise, in a questioning and frightened way.

Then the king-tiger made one last effort to show the cub, who thought he was a goat, what he really was. He put before the cub a piece of meat. At first the cub recoiled from it in horror. But then, coming closer, he tasted it. Suddenly his blood was warmed by it. And the tiger-cub, who thought he was a goat, lifted his head and set the jungle echoing with a mighty roar.

I have told you this story by Ramakrishnan because I think it says something about those two disciples on the road to Emmaus, and also something about ourselves. Like the tiger-cub, the disciples on the Emmaus road thought they knew who they were: ex-followers of a prophet from Nazareth. He was dead and they were disillusioned. They thought that they knew themselves for what they were—a couple of disappointed persons who had set their hearts on something which had failed. They were frustrated people who had tried something good, and it had ended in disaster. They were clearing out, to become ex-followers of Jesus of Nazareth. Like the tiger-cub, they preferred to go off and, as it were, bleat and munch grass. We too can have moments when we walk our Emmaus road, thinking we know who we really are—disillusioned, frustrated people, perhaps even on the point of becoming ex-followers of Jesus of Nazareth.

But for the disciples on the Emmaus road, and for us too, comes Christ the tiger. Out of the jungle of the night this burning tiger comes to tell us who we are, to reveal to us what we were made for. He first forces us, we tiger-cubs who think we are goats, to recognize our smallness, to see that we have been and are foolish and slow to believe. He thrusts before us our image.

But—curiously—we see ourselves only with him. We learn to look upon ourselves by looking also at the image of him who had first to suffer and thus enter into glory. In the mirror of Scripture we see Christ and ourselves, and become a little less foolish and not quite so slow to believe.

Only after we have begun to move from our unbelief and folly does Christ bring us to realize who he is and who we really are. The disciples knew him in the breaking of the bread. It is only when he warms our blood with the food he brought to us, that we really know who he is and who we truly are. It is only then that we can escape the limitations of our supposed goathood, and with a roar acknowledge the truth. Jesus, the king-tiger and revealer, must walk into our lives and show us precisely who we are by showing us who he is. The disciples on the Emmaus road were confronted with the risen Christ. But this happened only as they felt their hearts burning within them and found themselves on the road back to the community in Jerusalem. We too find ourselves when we find Christ and his community, or rather are found by him and them.

Like all great truths, it is a platitude that we discover ourselves in discovering others, above all in discovering others in love. The human "I" knows itself properly only in encountering a "Thou." It takes a life of I-Thou meetings to tell us who we are.

At the deepest level, we discover ourselves precisely in discovering ourselves before Christ. There is the true light which enlightens every man coming into the world. This light, whether explicitly identified or not, is Christ. "Know yourself" was one of the great slogans of Greek wisdom. But we will know ourselves finally, only if we know him. Strangers to Christ we remain strangers ultimately to ourselves. Without him we simply walk our Emmaus road thinking we know, when in fact we don't. We are so prone to be like the tiger-cub who considered himself to be a goat and was happy to be with the goats. Christ the tiger must come to tell us who we are. Come, Lord Jesus.

*Afterword*
*The Psychology*
*of The Second Journey*
*by Jack Dominian*

INTRODUCTION

Gerald O'Collins describes clearly and succinctly the phenomenon of a radical or modified change in the course of midlife which can have a range of effects from the profound to the substantial. He has shown that this is a possibility even though it is the transformation of major figures that catch and hold our attention. The important point of this book—and other contemporary thought—is that the 40's—60's are not primarily a concluding epoch but a period in which personal growth and change are part of its intrinsic course.

The traditional view of life with its emphasis on permanency and commitment in marriage or religious life tended to emphasize a static continuity. In fact we now know from psychological studies that the human person maintains a thread of similarity, a sense of continuing identity, which is easily recognised as personal and unique and yet this happens in the presence of continuous physical, intellectual, emotional, social and spiritual change.

The first fifteen years or so of life is the period when the foundations of the adult body, mind and feelings are laid down within the social and spiritual structures of the background of the home and the parents. In adolescence there is the culmination of the physical, intellectual, emotional and social differentiation between the young person and the parents. At this stage the young person is not yet a full adult but neither is he a child. The next few years are a period of rapid transition when adulthood is acquired with the advent of a commitment to work and a vocation of personal relationship. In the overwhelming majority of people this is to marriage, a small minority to the chosen state of celibacy and another small minority to the single state for a variety of voluntary or involuntary reasons. All this happens on an average in the early or mid twenties.

There follows a period of a decade or more until the mid-thirties when most men and women are busy settling into the role of workers, parents or the chosen single state. Most of their energy is consumed with outward events and activities. And then gradually and imperceptibly there is a shift to inner experiences which are primarily emotional. The point that needs making is that often the appearance of an urgent need to change course in midlife away from the familiar work, vocation or personal relationship has been preceded by changes and turbulence which may have proceeded for years within, without its true nature having been recognised. Indeed, in the forties there is another series of external events which hold the interest of everyone and which may temporarily divert attention from the inner world. These events are the menopause for women, the possibility of the death of one or both parents, the departure of children from home and their marriage and a critical stage being reached at work. Those in full-time work discover that they are not going to be promoted any further or they are promoted beyond their capacity to cope or they realise they are absolutely fed up with the work they are doing. All these external events are stations in the social journey of life which may either temporarily hide the inner turmoil or precipitate its outward manifestation.

The death of a parent may be the first intimate loss in life and lead to questioning of one's own ultimate end. The conclusion of the possibilities of promotion may suddenly shift emphasis away from power, status and gain and emphasize the trivial, uninspiring, boring job one has done for the last twenty years or more. The departure of children and the menopause may link up with the cessation of biological creativity and trigger off the need for alternative forms of creativity. All these events may, in fact, be the substitutes for an actual journey away from home and work, although the latter does occur frequently, as O'Collins says.

The central change of midlife is an inner one. It is intimately connected with feelings and ultimate values and it is those characteristics that need further probing. The changes may involve marked features in the personality which were powerfully affected in the first half of life; or they may be linked with an evolution of feelings that is more general and can involve everyone. These two categories need separate treatment.

## PROMINENT PERSONALITY TRAITS

Prominent personality traits which can be distorted in early life include trust, dependence, passivity and self-esteem and each one of them has its own characteristics.

### *Trust*

The ability to get close to another person and feel safe in their presence is a characteristic which is developed in the majority of children early in life. In the arms and on the knees of their parents they experience closeness and safe acceptance simultaneously so that thereafter they can allow themselves to reach and be reached intimately by others. There is a small group of men and women who are described as loners, as isolated persons, who find it difficult to get close to others. They may cope with their isolation by remaining single, marrying someone who is equally impersonal or entering a religious life which does not demand personal closeness. Alternatively, such a person may have multiple superficial relationships which stop when any form of closeness is attempted by the other person or any degree of trust is involved. Such personalities find it particularly difficult to disclose their inner world to others.

Gradually they find that their isolation is stifling and become aware of an overwhelming desire to get close to somebody else. The impersonal spouse may be discarded for another relationship of much greater emotional frankness. The religious life may be abandoned for a personal relationship of intimacy. Work which rarely allows close contact with individuals is given up for alternatives which demand close links with individuals. There is a need to get close and share one's inner world with another and he or she becomes the first significant other in life, including—for the first time—God, who may be the channel through which trust is attempted or established.

### Dependence

Everyone begins in utter physical, emotional, social and spiritual dependence. We need figures of authority who are stronger than ourselves to give us the means of survival. Ideally parents, teachers and others who guide our lives should be on the one hand supporting and on the other facilitating our development so that gradually we assume self-control and self-direction. There are, however, men and women who reach their twenties with a strong sense of dependence motivating their life. They are afraid to take charge of their own being and consciously or unconsciously find themselves in a relationship or situation of continuing dependence. They choose a spouse who is powerful, assertive and reliable, who continues the parental role. They enter a religious life which until recently emphasised obedience, the repudiation of one's self-direction and the value of absolute dependence on figures of authority. The Roman Catholic Church itself encouraged a widespread dependence of its people on figures of authority and indeed society as a whole was inclined to authoritarianism. Thus there was ample room for the emotionally dependent person to find leaders who were prepared to continue the role of crucial advisers.

The dependent person may remain so throughout life. A significant proportion, however, begin to emerge from their dependence in the mid-thirties to the fifties. Gradually they find the confidence to take increasing charge of their own life. They seek greater control over their destiny and they challenge authority. The differentiation from their surroundings, superiors or spouses takes place slowly but with increasing awareness that they are persons in their own right who no longer wish to live by kind permission of another. The implications are often startling. Unless the spouse can accommodate himself/herself to the newly discovered identity of their partner, they become increasingly confused as they no longer recognise the willing co-operation of the past. Spouses and superiors in religious life or at work are challenged and asked to recognise a new person. The challenge can be defiant or quietly assertive but a new life is certainly born whose resolution is implacable.

## Passivity

The dependent person may be passive but the passive person need not be dependent. A man or woman may feel shy, remain quiet, unobtrusive and let others handle initiatives. He or she is pleased to follow. But such outward passivity may hide an inner furnace of burning energy which gradually erupts. Men and women are promoted to offices and positions which transform them. The hesitant, indecisive man/woman gradually assumes initiative and authority and may take others by surprise at their hidden potential. The transformation may be overt. Silences are converted into an articulate outspokenness. Indecision is changed into discriminatory activity. Mistakes are made, of course, in the process: but the path is upwards towards greater confidence and the desire to undertake far more onerous tasks once the latent capacity has been discovered.

## Self-Esteem

The capacity to feel lovable, to offer and receive love is crucial to life and, in particular, to a full spiritual Christian life which is guided by the principle of love. There are countless men and women who grow up feeling uncertain of their worthiness, who find it very difficult to recognise and register love because they do not feel good enough. They serve and love others but find it very difficult to accept in return their own value. They long to be loved by men, women and God and yet emotionally cannot accept loving feelings. They may choose an undemonstrative spouse, who is more critical than affirmative. They may choose a religious life that stresses self-abnegation and they may pursue their insignificance in the false conviction that the greater their diminution the more worthy they will become spiritually.

Ultimately such a person may be filled with despair and the destructive desire to end it all as they contemplate their meaninglessness or become overwhelmed by their worthlessness. In all walks of life the self-rejecting person is to be found who, whilst full of talent, cannot feel any personal worth.

The second journey is often applicable to such a person. A chance encounter, a friendship, a journey, an inner dialogue with

God, some small event, an appreciative letter, psychiatry may, in fact, propel such a person through the gate of self-acceptance. Not that self-acceptance is sudden and complete at once. It continues throughout life. But the transformation from self-rejection to self-acceptance is the major event in that person's life.

It means that people can be approached without fear of their damaging critique or rejection. Rejection and acceptance of loving feelings from others becomes possible as personal worth is replenished and the depths of the resources to serve and love others increases. A breakthrough is made into the life of others who feel unloved and they too can now receive the persistent feeling of acceptance which may help them to break down their resistance. The absent or meaningless God can now enter our life, because we feel loved unconditionally. We cannot earn or deserve God's love and, so long as we tried to reach God in this way, there was an ever receding figure who could not be reached. But God now stands still and percolates inside an abode that finds room for the unfathomable without being agitated about its capacity to deserve or make welcome the ultimate source of love.

### General Traits

All the above traits are universal and yet afflict individuals to a greater or lesser extent. Those who have the more severe disorders find the second journey most clearly delineated. But there are other features of midlife which impinge upon all of us and need understanding.

### Destructiveness

Tho polarity between love and anger, facilitation and destructiveness is a prominent feature of all our personalities. Envy, jealousy, mistrust, power, success and greed, are all human features that mobilise anger, manipulation and control of others and so do lack of authenticity, lies, distortions of justice and denial of human rights. Most of our aggressivity, however, is not a deliberate choice. On the whole, human beings do not set out to destroy their neighbour. They do so often out of the conviction that, if they do not protect their own interests, others will exploit them. Our aggressivity is often a protection for our own vulnerabilities, fears and fantasies. These are often unconscious. We simply do not realise our envies, jealousies and anxieties and we are astonished when we find ourselves at the mercy of our aggression, protecting feelings we never knew were there. The fear of losing a spouse suddenly hits us as they flirt mildly with someone else. The full depth of our envy strikes us as somebody else gets the promotion, job or reward we were seeking. The capacity to be hurt out of misunderstanding, rejection or criticism makes itself clear as we find ourselves lashing out at a small provocation.

All this has been happening in the twenties and thirties and gradually we become aware of our dark, destructive side. The advent of greater security, self-acceptance and love of self and neighbour makes us gradually less vulnerable. We become aware of our resources and feel less threatened by others. We become aware of our fundamental goodness and can allow others to use us for their needs far more generously.

We become, in fact, much more clear about our dark, nasty, destructive side which no longer propels us around blindly. And, at the same time, we discover that on balance our capacity to love becomes greater than our drive to destroy. We find our strength, not through the bodies we walk over, but through the alliances of love we make.

Rarely, of course, is it our dark side that takes over. Aggression, hostility, destructiveness and power over others are the fruits of personal despair of ever feeling lovable and acceptable. If we feel we are never going to be loved for our own sake, then the only alternative is to make others our slaves through physical, emotional or social exploitation. Then our dark side gives full reign to its capacity to destroy rather than to love and there are men and women who see aggression as their only positive outlet.

Whatever part of the polarity reaches the surface, the consequences are monumental. When love conquers destructiveness then the ultimate of wholeness and holiness is on the way. When hatred and destruction become the governing influences, then other human beings become things to be used and discarded.

### Masculinity and Femininity

In our Western society we tend to associate masculinity with physical strength, reassurance, executive potential, aggressivity and

93

the manifestation of will power. The feminine tends to be associated with gentleness, feelings and emotions, intuitiveness, the aesthetic, the passive, receptive and creative. A great deal of this is socially determined; but part of it is drawn from the biological differences. From time immemorial, however, it has been recognised that the sexes contain an admixture of both masculine and feminine characteristics. And, indeed, with the passage of time men tend to become more gentle, less aggressive, more inclined to let their feelings and emotions speak to them and are ruled less by reason and will and more by their intuitive insights which are called experience. Women, on the other hand, tend to assume more authority, become more assertive and authoritative with the passage of time and feel able to take charge of responsibilities which need a lot of reasoning, will-power and decision. These are all changes which may be pronounced in individual men and women and less so in others. In fact, as social changes associated with the emancipation of women become more marked, there is likelihood of an earlier evidence of admixture of qualities. Women are taking upon themselves to demonstrate they do not lack male qualities and men are far freer to express themselves in less rigid masculine forms. The masculine, in fact, often finds its home in collectivities, in groups of people who are managed and directed. The feminine is far more personal, individualistic and deals with the affective side of life. Men are increasingly becoming nurses, social workers and join other personal services, whilst women are seeking and obtaining executive posts that control groups of persons.

It is in the midst of life, however, that the balance of the two characteristics finds an acceptance which is not burdened by social embarrassment. Men can relax and show their feeling, caring side far more easily and women can show their capacities to initiate, take charge, control, plan without worrying about their femininity. These changes, of course, may and do mean that men will change their jobs in mid career, leaving behind executive posts and becoming priests, social officers, probation officers and other similar vocations whilst women may take charge of offices, businesses and other executive positions.

### Wisdom

In terms of our absolute resources we tend to reach the peaks of our physical and intellectual potential in our late teens. But in terms of growth we have a lifetime in front of us to transform our resources into powerful sources of wisdom. The physically gifted become, with time, athletes of excellence. Our intellectual resources are refined with reflection, evaluation and discrimination and gradually converted into wisdom. Our social resources gradually lose the need to impress people by putting on an inscrutable social mask and allow our genuine, authentic sense of ourselves to emerge. These are the moments when we begin to break with precedent and act—not with social prudence—but with the spontaneity that springs from the depths of our being. We don't quite know why we have said or done something or reacted in a particular way: we know immediately that it was the right response or initiative which challenged our accepted social image, but reflected much more accurately our humanity and, perhaps for the first time, our hidden generosity, compassion, care and concern. We feel free to break the taboos and barriers of social expectation and be ourselves.

This ability to do justice to our inner being may have profound impact on our work and relationships. We may have harboured desires from our childhood or adolescence to farm, to be an artist, to write, to take up music, to see the world, to take up a special hobby and now we feel free and have the insight to realise this is the moment of a second career.

With the growth of our wisdom and the less critical and destructive attitude to others, our view of other human beings can become much more gentle and benevolent. We can understand far more the reasons for their behaviour even though we do not approve of it. We become far more tolerant and accepting and find that these features are far more permissive than the insistence of right and wrong and the rigidity of the law.

Reconciliation within ourselves and towards others become the marks of the transformation.

### The Waiting Period

The description of the change given above suggests a rapidity of movement from one state to another which is not cumbersome or difficult to negotiate. It is true that some of these insights may come as a flash of illumination. Other changes, however, may proceed very slowly and painfully. The important point to be made, however, is this. Whether the conscious awareness and change is

95

slow and deliberate or the result of being seized by a force within or without which baffles explanation and demands instant acknowledgement, the fact remains that for a long time men and women, in the course of change, can remain in a vacuum. Their feelings, ideas and outlook are attached to the past with its familiar pattern of behaviour whilst their inner being is moving towards a new pattern of feelings, ideas and outlook. For a period of time, which may last months or years, they may remain utterly confused. Sheer habit may draw them to the past and the new forces incline them to new and unknown patterns which they have to learn for the first time. During the alteration they may not know who they are and where they are going, even if they know where they have come from. In this state of apparent emptiness and confusion there are two certainties. One is the feeling that one cannot go back, however tempting it is to do so. And the second is the need to open ourselves to the help of God to see us through. This is truly a journey of forward conviction, led in a blind way, with the hand thrust in that of God, that the ultimate destination will be reached.

A great deal of spiritual awakening occurs in these middle years as change opens within us a vacuum that needs God to fill it and ourselves to preserve and retain its meaning.

### Authenticity

The authenticity of the journey will be found in the imperative pressure to proceed forward. The past, however attractive, is no longer meaningful to us. We have a compelling sense to change in our feelings, attitudes and sometimes our work. Often we don't change anything, neither work nor personal circumstances nor our vocation. Instead everything we do and relate begins to take on a new meaning. This new meaning may lead us to uncertainty, to doubt, to anxiety, to depression but, as long as it is authentic, it will not leave us alone. In our conscious thoughts, dreams and fantasies we live in an atmosphere of inner turbulence that compels transformation. And strangely, in the midst of the unknown and unrecognised, there is a feeling of peace. We have found ourselves at last and we are not really surprised that this is happening to us. It feels that what we are discovering now has always been a part of ourselves, which in the past was an unrealisable dream. Now it is a possibility which we can't let go.

There is a force inside which bothers us with its truth, however hard and tough the reality we are attempting may appear. And often we feel we are no longer alone, a force beyond description has seized us and is moving us forward, whose impetus we can neither understand nor dare to ignore. Authenticity will be found in the midst of all this atmosphere for its very essence will be that which frightens, suppresses and represses others, acts as a catalyst for necessary growth in us. The authenticity of change will be found in its inspiration, determination and commitment to alteration without knowing the destination. It is a metamorphosis that joins faith, hope and love in an I-Thou encounter with self, neighbour and God.

# Notes

*Preface*

1. This unpublished dissertation in English literature dealt with the works of Joseph Conrad, Tobias George Smollett and other writers. Hereafter this dissertation will be referred to as "Puzon." See also Sr. Puzon's "The Hidden Meaning in *Humphry Clinker*," *Harvard Library Bulletin*, 24 (1976), pp. 40–54. I wish to thank her also for drawing my attention to Bunyan, Dante, T. S. Eliot, the *Aeneid* and the *Odyssey*.
2. New York, 1976.
3. C. G. Jung, *Psychological Reflections: A New Anthology of His Writings*, ed. J. Jacobi (London: 1971), pp. 137–38; hereafter *Psychological Reflections*.
4. Puzon, chapter I.


*Chapter One*

1. *Face to Face* (New York: 1976), p. vi.
2. Puzon, pp. 2 and 95.
3. *Ibid.*, p. 192.
4. London: 1969, pp. 57–58.
5. Puzon, pp. 2a and 23.


*Chapter Two*

1. Gordon Wakefield in *Fire of Love* (London: 1976) indicates the sources for the material on Wesley.
2. *New York*, August 30, 1976, p. 28.
3. *The Autobiography of St. Ignatius Loyola*, trans. J. F. O'Callaghan and ed. J. C. Olin (New York: 1974), pp. 3–4.

4. The material from Bonhoeffer's diary and other quotations come from Eberhard Bethge, *Dietrich Bonhoeffer* (English trans.; New York: 1970), pp. 552–66 and *Gesammelte Schriften*, I (Munich: 1965), pp. 279–354.

5. All quotations come from Malcolm Muggeridge, *Something Beautiful for God* (London: 1972).


## Chapter Three

1. Puzon, p. 87.

2. *Ibid.*, pp. 22–24. For the distinction between the inner and the outer journey, see *ibid.*, p. 14 and chapter I (*passim*).

3. For this and the following paragraph I am indebted to conversations with Sr. Puzon; see also her dissertation, p. 7, and an article by her to appear in the *Harvard Library Bulletin* for 1978.


## Chapter Four

1. Puzon, p. 15. In the context of the theology of hope, I distinguished between Aeneids and Odysseys on the basis that, unlike Ulysses, "Aeneas did not voyage back to his home and family, but sailed on to a new and open future" (my review of W.H. Capps, *From Cathedrals to Ships, Interpretation* 26 (1972), p. 476.

2. London: 1970, p. 83.


## Chapter Five

1. Fr. Joseph Goetz provided me with the story from Ramakrishnan. Once again I wish to acknowledge gratefully his kindness.